And They Rode On

1st King's Dragoon Guards at Waterloo
Oil painting by R. Caton Woodville

And They Rode On

THE KING'S DRAGOON GUARDS
AT WATERLOO

———

MICHAEL MANN

MICHAEL RUSSELL

TO CAPTAIN PHILIP ASHLEY MANN

IST THE QUEEN'S DRAGOON GUARDS

Killed in Action 13 April 1975

© Michael Mann 1984

First published in Great Britain 1984
by Michael Russell (Publishing) Ltd
The Chantry, Wilton, Salisbury, Wiltshire

Designed by Humphrey Stone

Set in Sabon by The Spartan Press Ltd, Lymington
Printed and bound in Great Britain
by Billings of Worcester

ISBN 0 85955 111 3

Contents

List of Maps and Illustrations

Maps drawn by Ray Smith

Foreword

'We are King's Dragoon Guards – not Royals,' shouted a small party of cavalrymen on being ordered to rally and form by an officer of the Royal Dragoons after a charge at Waterloo; 'and they rode on.'

This deep sense of regimental pride and loyalty has been the glory of the British Army for 300 years, and the envy of many a foreign soldier. This book tells the story of one regiment – the 1st King's Dragoon Guards – during the Waterloo Campaign, as seen through the eyes of serving members of that senior cavalry regiment of the line.

Since 1945 a series of documents and letters written by members of the King's Dragoon Guards who served during the campaign have come to light. They range from Captain James Naylor's Troop Diary, to letters written home by Lieutenant Hibbert, Troop Sergeant Major Page, Corporal Stubbings and Private Charles Stanley, to a poem composed by Trumpeter Samuel Wheeler and reminiscences by Captain Wallace. Given the lack of education and the general standard of literacy of the period, it is extraordinary that such a collection of eyewitness accounts, drawn from right across the social spectrum, should have survived from one regiment. And for the most part they have remained generally unknown for 150 years.

I have relied mainly upon these KDG sources, but not entirely; for where there are other contemporary eyewitness accounts – for instance, by members of the Household Cavalry Brigade, or by troops who were attached to that Brigade or who were nearby, as was Mercer of the Royal Horse Artillery – these form a useful additional source of information without detracting from the main purpose of following the campaign through the eyes and experience of one regiment.

I have not attempted to describe the course of the various engagements in detail, and have only given such a general account as will make the narrative intelligible to the general reader. The soldier engaged in battle never sees the whole of it; he only remembers that part in which he and his regiment were involved. But his experience is always a vivid one, and these Waterloo accounts, told in the language of the time, help re-create for us the feel and the atmosphere of those tremendous days.

The 1st King's Dragoon Guards was raised in 1685, and after 273 years of service was amalgamated with the 2nd Dragoon Guards, the Queen's Bays, in 1958, to form the present regiment, 1st The Queen's Dragoon Guards. Both the KDG and the Bays were old friends and had fought together under Marlborough, and in more recent times in the Western Desert and Italy. The combined regiment has carried on the joint traditions of its two illustrious parents, and still remains essentially a 'family' regiment, where son often succeeds father in service to the Crown.

I am particularly grateful to Major R. Hollies Smith, my lifelong friend and, like myself, an old KDG, for so many valuable suggestions and so much help. I am also grateful to Boris Mollo of the National Army Museum, and Colonel Newton of the Army Museums Ogilby Trust for their help as well as their permission to quote from material within their care. I acknowledge my thanks to Leo Cooper for permission to quote from his father's book *British Regular Cavalry*, from Eversley Belfield's history of 1st The Queen's Dragoon Guards and from Ugo Pericole's *Armies at Waterloo*; and to Brian Robson similarly for reference to his classic *Swords of the British Army*. I am also grateful to Messrs Sidgwick and Jackson for permission to quote from Lord Chalfont's *Waterloo*, to Jonathan Cape to use material from the Marquess of Anglesey's *One-Leg*, and to William Collins for reference to David Howarth's *A Near Run Thing*. I am grateful to my fellow Trustees of the Regimental Museum of 1st The Queen's Dragoon Guards for permission to quote from the sources in their care. Above all, I must thank Lieutenant Colonel John Hibbert for his generous permission to quote so extensively from John Hibbert's letters, and Trumpeter Wheeler's poem.

Again, my thanks and gratitude must go to the Commanding Officer of 1st The Queen's Dragoon Guards for permission to reproduce two paintings which now hang in the Officers' Mess; to the Army Museums Ogilby Trust for the portrait of an unknown officer; to Major R. Hollies Smith for the painting of Major Graham, and the French artist's impression of a KDG; to Mrs Margaret Birley for the portrait of James Leatham; to my fellow Trustees of the Regimental Museum of 1st The Queen's Dragoon Guards for the portrait of Captain Sterling; and my humble duty to Her Majesty The Queen for her gracious permission to reproduce two watercolours by Langendyk and one by Krausz now in the Royal Library at Windsor Castle.

Finally, I must thank Miss Christine Seaman and Mrs Caroline Balcon for their patience and industry in typing the manuscript, and Michael Russell for coping so readily with all the many problems that inevitably arise. Without their cheerful help and encouragement, and the constant support of my wife, this book would never have been written.

Windsor 1984   MICHAEL MANN

ONE

Arrival in the Low Countries

16 APRIL TO 16 JUNE 1815

Napoleon had escaped from the island of Elba. His arrival in Paris on 20 March 1815 marked the beginning of the 'Hundred Days' that spanned the Waterloo campaign and brought his final downfall. In Vienna the news of his landing in France had brought a pledge from Great Britain, Russia, Austria and Prussia each to put 150,000 men into the field. Command of the British army was given to the Duke of Wellington, but with the superb Peninsular army now disbanded and many of its most experienced troops still in America, it was a matter of hastily cobbling together what was available.

The 1st King's Dragoon Guards were serving at home and were increased from an establishment of ten troops numbering 726 all ranks to one of twelve troops totalling 1,148 officers and men. In early April orders were received for 27 officers and 505 non-commissioned officers and men, together with 537 horses, to move to the Low Countries under command of Lieutenant Colonel William Fuller, to join the army being assembled around Brussels.[1] The eight troops forming the four squadrons marched from their quarters and embarked at Tilbury, Purfleet and Gravesend on 16 April.[2] After one night spent lying off Southend and another in Margate Roads, they arrived off Ostend on the 19th, lay another day off Ostend for lack of sufficient depth of water and disembarked on the 20th. The regiment then proceeded by easy marches to quarters around Ghent,[3] where it remained for a few days, and then to billets in the Dender valley.[4] Colonel Fuller, who had been looking after affairs in London, joined the regiment on 27 April.[3] Regimental headquarters was established at St Levens Esche with troops billeted around at Eygam, Liederkerke,[5] Nyderhasselt, Aloste[3] and Denderleur.[2]

King's Dragoon Guards leaving their billets in Kent.

The Household Cavalry Brigade, forming the 1st Brigade of British cavalry, under command of Major General Lord Edward Somerset and consisting of two squadrons each of the 1st and 2nd Life Guards and the Royal Horse Guards, was weak in numbers, and so the four squadrons of the 1st King's Dragoon Guards were added to the six squadrons of the Household Cavalry to bring the brigade up to strength. Sir Henry Torrens, Military Secretary to the Duke of York, wrote to the Duke of Wellington on 21 April: 'In reference to what I said to you respecting the inefficiency in numbers of the Household Cavalry Brigade, four Squadrons of the 1st Dragoon Guards have been ordered to be attached to it.'[6] It is noteworthy, in view of the attention given to the subsequent exploits of the Household Cavalry, that of the 1,349 sabres mustered in the brigade at Waterloo, 530 were King's Dragoon Guards, almost forty per cent of the total.[6]

The month of May spent in billets in the Dender valley gave the officers and men a chance to gauge the feelings of the local populace – though most of the wealthier locals were absent – and to see something of the countryside. The Belgians much preferred the English to the Prussians, whom they detested and feared, but they seemed ready enough to believe some ridiculous rumours. Wellington was said to have been placed under arrest and sent home to be court-martialled for helping Napoleon escape from Elba, and for being in constant communication with him since; further, he had agreed to surrender the British army in return for large sums of money, and had given up his religion provided Bonaparte would make him King of Naples. Many French-speaking Belgians were sympathetic to the Napoleonic cause, and could not believe that God would allow that the Emperor could escape from Elba only to be beaten and imprisoned again, especially by soldiers who were not even Catholics. As Lieutenant Hibbert KDG commented: 'It is well they cannot make themselves understood to the soldiers, or it might prejudice their minds greatly, for there are many Irish Regiments here and all Roman Catholics.'[2]

The two months spent in Belgium before hostilities commenced were filled with regimental duties, and with sightseeing and purchases for the officers of the regiment. Captain Naylor KDG notes a succession of parades and watering orders, and on 20 May and on 4, 9 and 15 June there were field days. He notes, too, disciplinary matters. He attended a court martial of two privates of Captain Sweeney's troop at regimental headquarters on Sunday 7 May, and their punishment at 7 a.m. the following day. He also attended two more punishment parades at 5 a.m. and 6 a.m. respectively on 12 and 14 June.[3] In late April or early May, John Hibbert witnessed the first flogging since the regiment left Clonmel in Ireland in 1814. He escaped a similar duty because of a riding accident, which laid him up and also kept him away from the actions on 16, 17 and 18 June at Quatre Bras and Waterloo. 'I got off an unpleasant duty, which is seeing four men flogged tomorrow for getting drunk on duty. One of them in a frolick loaded his carbine with three ball cartridges, one on the other, and very deliberately shot at the other three who were before in order, as he said, to let them hear the noise the balls made in passing. It was lucky that none of them were killed.'[2] Naylor tells us the name of the offender was Private William

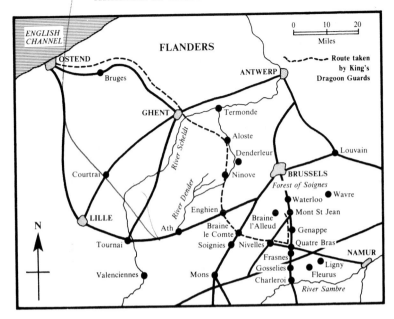

Marvin of No. 6 Troop, who had enlisted in the King's Dragoon Guards at the age of sixteen on 2 June 1806.[3]

Early in May a final inspection of arms, accoutrements and clothing took place, when all deficiencies were made good, and all old blankets and kit were taken into store and packed up into bales for despatch back to Ostend. The heavy baggage was placed in store at Ghent on 10 May.[6] Officers kept a look-out for horses, and Naylor purchased a bat-horse (for carrying his baggage) for fifteen Napoleons, and Hibbert did the same for £15. But as an officer's forage allowance only covered three horses, the cost of feeding these additional animals had to be met from their own pockets.[2,3]

The horse lines were on the whole excellent. 'The horses were living in clover, for their racks and mangers were full of it, and their stalls of clean straw up to their bellies, though this bounty was in some measure repaid by the manure, which was so valuable that the production of one horse in twenty-four hours was worth at least three or four pounds of hay and perhaps four times the quantity of clover.'[6]

4

On the subject of weapons James Smithies of the Royal Dragoons reminds us that the sword issued to the heavy cavalry at this period was not satisfactory; its straight blade made it ineffective for cutting and its hatchet point rendered it useless for thrusting. In this period before Waterloo, Smithies writes, 'for the first time ever known in the Army, the cavalry were ordered to grind the backs of their swords' – to a point.[7]

If the officers were able to shop, see the local sights and dine with neighbours, life was harder for the private soldier. On 15 May Private Charles Stanley, writing from 'Brusels Flemish Flanders' as 'Privert King's Dragoon Guards' to his cousin, describes the lot of the ordinary trooper:

Dear Couson,

I take this oppetunety of riting to you hoping this will find you all in good helth as it leaves me at present – I thank God for it – I have had a very ruf march since I saw you at Booton – We are onley 15 miles from Mr. Boney Part Harmey wish we expect to have a rap at him exerry day – We have the most Cavilrey of the English that ever was none at one time and in gud condishon and gud sperrits – We have lost a few horses by hour marshing – I have the pleasure to say my horse is better everry day whish I think im to be the best friend I have at presant – There is no dout of us beting the confounded rascal – it ma cost me my life and a meaney more that will onley be the forting of war – my life I set no store by at all – this is the finiest countrey exer is so far before England – the peepel is so sivel.

We have one good thing cheep – that it tabaco and everrything a Corduley Tabaco is 4d per lb – Gin is 1s.8d. per galland that is 2½ per quart – and everrything in perposion – hour alounse per day is one pound of beef and pound and half of bred – half a pint of gin – But the worst of all we dont get it regeler and if we dont get it the day it is due we luse it – wish is often the case I assure you – I hope you will never think of being a soldier – I assure you it is a verry ruf consern – I have rote to my sister Ann and I ham afraid she thinks the trubel to mush to anser.

I have not ad the pleasure of liing in a bed since in the cuntrey –

thank God the weather is fine wish is in hour faver – we get no pay at all onley hour bed and mete and gin – we have had 1od per day soped from us wish we shal reseive wen six months is expiered – I thank God I have a frend with me.

I hope you will excuse my bad inditing and spelling.[8]

At this period there cannot have been many private soldiers who were literate. Private Charles Stanley's letter conveys vividly the feelings and the deep patriotism of the ordinary soldier of the period. He was wrong about his pay, as Captain James Naylor records in his diary that he received some pay for his troop on 5 June, and more on the 11th, which made up the pay for the troop to 24 June. Poor Stanley's graver forebodings, however, were fulfilled. He fell in action on the field of Waterloo.

On Saturday 6 May Lieutenant General the Earl of Uxbridge, commanding the British cavalry, inspected the regiment and on 21 May his orders read that 'the appearance of the Household Brigade was excellent', and that he had 'not the smallest doubt that every individual would continue to exert the utmost zeal towards maintaining that order and discipline which must enable the regiments to perform the most important services which can be required'.[6] Another review of the British cavalry by the Prince of Orange took place on 24 May at Heldingem, involving the two brigades of heavy cavalry. The two regiments of Life Guards, the Blues, Inniskillings and Greys were inspected along with the King's Dragoon Guards, although the 1st Dragoons had not at that time arrived in Belgium.[3] The brother of the Bourbon King Louis, the Duc de Berri, commented that his brother could not but be re-established in his possessions when he had so excellent a body of forces to assist him.[2] After this inspection the King's Dragoon Guards were moved into billets around Ninove. A much grander review was held on Monday 29 May, when Wellington and Marshal Blücher, accompanied by the Duc de Berri and many other distinguished personages, inspected the whole of the British cavalry. This review took place near Grammont in the meadows by the banks of the Dender, for the use of which Mercer claims that the sum of £400 to £500 was paid.[5] The regiments reviewed were the 1st and 2nd Life Guards, the Blues, and King's Dragoon Guards of the Household Cavalry Brigade; the 1st Royal Dragoons, Greys and Inniskillings of the 2nd or Union Brigade, under Major General Sir William Ponsonby; the 23rd Light Dragoons of the 3rd (Light) Cavalry Brigade under Major General William Dornberg; the 11th, 12th and 16th Light Dragoons of the 4th Brigade under Major General Sir John Vandeleur; the 5th Hussar Brigade of 7th and 15th Hussars and the 13th Light Dragoons under Major General Sir Colquhoun Grant; and finally the 10th and 18th Hussars in the 6th Cavalry Brigade under Major General Sir Hussey Vivian. In addition there were eight batteries of the Royal Horse Artillery present.[2,3,5,9] Not on parade were the cavalry regiments of the King's German Legion, comprising the 1st and 2nd Light Dragoons, and the 1st, 2nd and 3rd Regiments of Hussars, who made up the strengths of the 3rd, 6th and 7th Cavalry Brigades.

The review took place between the villages of Jedeghem and Schendelbeke. The cavalry were formed up in three lines. The first line along the banks of the River Dender was composed of Hussars with wide intervals between squadrons, and a battery of 9-pounders on either flank. The second line was made up of the heavy cavalry, including the King's Dragoon Guards, with only the usual squadron intervals, with a battery of 24-pounder howitzers and 9-pounders in the centre, and two more batteries of 9-pounders on each flank. The third line was also formed with close intervals and was composed of Light Dragoons with a 9-pounder battery on each flank. Mercer describes the scene: 'The day was lovely and it was a splendid spectacle. The scattered lines of Hussars in their fanciful, yet picturesque costumes; the more sober, but far more imposing, line of heavy Dragoons, like a wall of red brick; and again the serviceable and active appearance of the third line in their blue uniforms, with broad lappels of white, buff, red, yellow and orange – the whole backed by the dark wood – formed indeed a fine picture.'[5]

The day did not pass without a diplomatic upset, which well shows the indifference the British soldier had for anything not British, and especially his contempt and lack of respect for the

Bourbons. 'Arriving on the ground covered with dust, the different corps had no sooner formed in their position, and dismounted, than off went belts, canteens and haversacks, and a general brushing and scrubbing commenced – for the Duke, making no allowance for dusty or muddy roads, expected to see all as clean as if just turned out: accordingly, we had not only brought brushes etc., but even straw to wisp over the horses. The whole line was in the midst of this business, many of the men even jackets off – when suddenly a forest of plumes and a galaxy of brilliant uniforms came galloping down the slope from Schendel-beke towards the temporary bridge [built over the Dender in the centre of the line]. "The Duke!, the Duke!, the Duke's coming!," rang along the lines, and for a moment caused considerable bustle amongst the people; but almost immediately this was discovered to be a mistake, and the brushing and cleaning recommenced with more devotion than ever; whilst the cavalcade, after slowly descending to the bridge and debouching on the meadows, started at full gallop toward the saluting point already marked out, the Duc de Berri (brother of King Louis), whom we now recognized, keeping several yards ahead, no doubt that he might clearly be seen. At this point he reined up and looked haughtily and impatiently around him; and as we were now pretty intimate with his manner it was easy to see that he was in a passion. The brushing, however, suffered no interruption, and no notice was taken of his presence. One of his suite was now called up and despatched to the front. The messenger no sooner returned than his Highness was off like a comet, his tail streaming after him all the way up the slope, unable to keep pace with him, for he rode like a madman, whilst a general titter pervaded our lines as the report flew from one to the other that Monnseer was off in a huff because we did not give him a general salute.'[5]

Wellington and Blücher arrived on the field at one o'clock, and were received with a salute of nineteen guns. The entourage rode down the lines inspecting the cavalry and horse artillery; their appearance drew general admiration. The Duke then placed himself at the centre of the first line, and the regiments passed by him in review in columns of half squadrons. John Hibbert

*1st King's Dragoon Guards private in the uniform worn
at Waterloo, except that overalls were worn on service
instead of breeches and jackboots.*

describes the scene in a letter to his sister: 'You may conceive
what a sight it was when a line was composed of sixteen regiments
of cavalry, and all in the most beautiful condition imaginable.
This line was exactly three miles in extent – a comfortable sight
for the French rascals had they been there. Marshal Blücher was
highly delighted, and all the foreigners who were present. Lord
Wellington made his appearance at one o'clock and did not

9

dismiss us until six, so we had had quite enough of it by the time we got home, which was about nine. We were altogether about fifteen hours on horseback, and nothing to eat or drink; added to this it was the hottest day I ever felt and many men fainted in the ranks. There were also many accidents such as broken legs, arms, and some horses killed. The Thirteenth got bogged on the Common, and I saw no less than fifteen men and horses down together, not including lots of upsets which invariably happen on these occasions. I did not hear of any men being killed. The only accident WE had, was in my troop as we were on the march there. One of the privates, being in a rage with his horse for not walking, hit him such a violent blow with his fist on the head that he broke his own arm. He deserved it most richly, and I told him by way of comfort that I was truly as glad at what had happened.'[2]

Thursday 15 June was a field day for two of the KDG squadrons, but it was to be the last day of routine soldiering. Before dawn on the 16th orders were received for the regiment to assemble at Ninove with the utmost despatch.

TWO

Quatre Bras and the Retreat to Mont St Jean

16 TO 18 JUNE 1815

'We were comfortably situated in Flanders, in good quarters wanting for nothing, till the morning of June 16th, when at daylight we received a sudden order to march.' So wrote Troop Sergeant Major Page in a letter home dated 3 July 1815.[10] Captain James Naylor's diary records: 'Before daybreak received an order to assemble at Ninove with all expedition.'[3]

Reports of the French advance had led the Duke of Wellington to issue a first set of orders between 5 p.m. and 7 p.m. on the 15th, placing the troops in a state of readiness. A second set of orders was issued at 10 p.m., following reports of the capture of Charleroi by the French and requests for news of the Duke's intentions from Marshal Blücher The British cavalry under Lord Uxbridge were ordered to march on Enghien, a town a few miles to the west of Quatre Bras. These orders did not reach the King's Dragoon Guards until 3 a.m. on the 16th, and the task of concentrating the troops took some time, scattered as they were over a range of billets in the hamlets and villages of the Dender valley.[6] But by 8 a.m. the regiment was paraded at Ninove. There was a wait of an hour before moving off along with the 1st and 2nd Life Guards and the Blues[3] of the 1st Heavy Cavalry (or Household) Brigade, commanded by Lord Edward Somerset.

With so many columns of cavalry converging, progress was very slow along the narrow roads with their high hedges. Enghien was passed by on the right and the brigade was ordered to push on for Braine le Comte, which was reached by 4 p.m. There the regiment was halted in close column and allowed to dismount. An hour's rest was granted for watering and food. The march so far had been under a burning sun, and men and horses were parched and ravenous. It seemed that the nose-bags were scarcely on the horses' heads when at 5 p.m. the order came to mount and move off. Mercer, whose horse artillery battery was attached to the Household Brigade, wrote: 'Many of the houses of the town had a sort of gallery behind them, which were filled with spectators, particularly many priests. The gardens were very pretty, and I could not but contrast the comparative luxury of these people, snug and comfortable, and sure of their bed when night came on, with our own vagabond situation.'[5]

The regiment now pressed on towards Nivelles through rich and wooded country that extended to an abrupt ridge of hills which was covered with forest. When they reached the long straggling street of the village of Long Tour at the foot of the hills, they found it choked with baggage and waggons, holding up the march. The brigade was ordered to break into the fields.[6] The road now ran through hilly country bordered by trees on either side, and then began to degenerate into a zigzag little better than a track. At last the cavalry rode onto a high plateau covered still with forest, but with an occasional clearing and a few fields. As the King's Dragoon Guards emerged from the forest, Captain Naylor tells us: 'We heard a cannonade and at times could distinctly see a smoke at some distance.'[3]

At once the order was given to proceed at a brisk trot. In order to lighten their horses, the men untied the nets containing hay and also opened the mouths of the feed-bags, 'which falling from them as they trotted on, the road was soon covered with hay and oats.'[6,11] As they reached Nivelles, the sound 'became more distinct, and its character was no longer questionable – heavy firing of cannon and musketry, which could now be distinguished from each other plainly. We could also hear the musketry in volleys and independent firing. The extensive view below us was bounded towards the horizon by a dark line of woods, above which, in the direction of the cannonade, volumes of grey smoke arose, leaving no doubt what was going on. The object of our march was now evident, and we commenced descending the long slope with an animation we had not felt before.'[5]

It was now 7 p.m. as the brigade descended the straight slope towards Nivelles, 'which lay spread out before us – its towers and masses of building, especially what appeared to be the ruins of an ancient castle, sweetly touched by the golden light of the setting sun, whilst the greater part lay in deep-toned purple obscurity. Beyond the town the ground rose, also in shadowy obscurity, crowned with sombre woods over which ascended the greyish-blue smoke of the battle, now apparently so near that we fancied we could hear the shouts of the combatants – a fancy strengthened by crowds of people on the heights, whom we mistook for troops – inhabitants of Nivelles, as we soon discovered, seeking to get a sight of the fearful tragedy then enacting.'[5]

As the cavalry entered Nivelles they found that 'the whole population was in the streets, doors and windows all wide open, whilst the inhabitants stood huddled together in little groups like frightened sheep, or were hurrying along with the distracted air of people uncertain where they are going, or what they are doing.'[5] Many wounded were arriving and Captain Naylor learnt that the action had started at 4 p.m. General Picton's division had borne the brunt of the fighting and, along with the Belgian troops, had many casualties. The 1st Foot (Royal Scots), the 42nd, the 44th and 92nd of Pack's brigade had been repeatedly charged by the French cavalry, and Kempt's brigade, consisting of the 28th, 32nd, 79th and 95th Regiments, had suffered heavily at the hands of the French cuirassiers.[3]

Excited civilians would 'run up and patting our horses' necks, bid us hasten to the fight ere it were yet too late, or utter trembling and not loud shouts of "Vivent les Anglais". A few there were who stood apart, with gloomy discontented looks, eyeing their fellow citizens with evident contempt, and us with scowls, not minimised with derision, as they marked our dusty and jaded appearance.'[5]

The brigade pressed on and, climbing the hill beyond the town, they met 'a fine chausée bordered by elms, expecting every moment to enter on the field of action, the roar of which appeared quite close to us.'[5] It was, however, still some way off. They now began to meet numerous Dutch or Belgian soldiers, many of them wounded, but as many apparently untouched. Furthermore, the wounded were attended by six, eight, ten and even sometimes more able-bodied soldiers. When asked about the progress of the battle and why they had left the field, the unabashed answer came: 'Tout est perdu, les Anglais sont abimés, en déroute, abimés, tous, tous, tous!' At last a solitary private of the Gordon Highlanders came limping along, a musket ball lodged in his knee. 'Na, na, sir, it's aw a damned lee. They was fechtin gat an I left em; but it's a bluidy business, and thar's na saying fat may be the end on't. Oor regiment was nigh clean swept off, and oor Colonel kilt just as I came awa.'[5]

Dusk began to close in as the brigade trotted through the village of Hautain Le Val and beyond it reached the edge of the battlefield after a march of nearly fifty miles. In the gathering dark horses stumbled from time to time over the corpses lying in the road. It was now 8 p.m., and the firing had nearly ceased. The King's Dragoon Guards formed a close column by the side of the road, where they stood for about an hour before marching to a bivouac in an open field among the remains of a crop of wheat, well in front of Genappe and to the rear of the farmhouse of Quatre Bras. The horses were picketed but were kept linked in column, saddled and bridled, as the French were occupying a large wood about two miles in front of their position.[3]

As soon as the troopers were dismounted every available man was sent with canteen and buckets to fetch water at a well in the farm. This was apparently the only source immediately at hand and so great was the crush of all arms that watering the horses took several hours. They had been fed with what corn remained when a patch of standing corn was discovered, which was pulled up or cut and fed to the tired animals. Then the officers and men stood or lay by their horses through a fine summer night, some chatting and listening to the noise and confusion around the well, some trying to snatch some sleep, enveloped in their cloaks.

Of the six British cavalry brigades, only one regiment, the 11th Hussars, the leading regiment of Vandeleur's brigade, had managed to reach the field whilst the battle was still in progress, and they only arrived at the very end of the day in the fading light.

Unidentified officer of 1st King's Dragoon Guards, c.1812.

Sergeant Major Page noted: 'We marched this day 40 English miles and slept in the open corn-fields, our horses being saddled ready to mount at a minute's notice, the French being in a wood close by us.'[10]

The night passed quietly until about an hour before sunrise, when a British cavalry patrol found itself by accident between the enemy's pickets near the farm of Piramont. The French raised an alarm, and fired on the patrol. The firing rapidly extended along the line of outposts on both sides. But as both French and British officers realised that it was only a brush with a patrol, the spluttering musketry ceased, confidence was restored and with daylight quiet descended on both armies.[6] Sergeant Major Page recorded that 'on the morning of the 17th at daybreak firing again commenced. So far it was what we call skirmishing.'[10]

Daylight revealed the evidence of the previous day's battle. The corn was trampled down, and the ground in front covered with the bodies of the dead and wounded. To the immediate front of the farm of Quatre Bras there were heaps of bodies of Highlanders, cuirassiers and horses. The light blue and orange facings of the dead cuirassiers showed them to be from the 8th and 11th Cuirassiers of Guiton's brigade. Kellermann, taunted by Marshal Ney, had led this brigade himself, twenty paces in front of the leading squadron. They had charged in column of squadrons, each squadron separated by an interval double its own front; so they fell on the British centre held by the 42nd, 79th and 92nd Highlanders of Picton's division. The line held, but not before many Highlanders had fallen, and the colours of the 69th Regiment of Alten's division were captured, as the regiment was caught by the Cuirassiers in line and cut to pieces, due to an error of judgment by the young Prince of Orange.

Soon after daybreak the Duke of Wellington, having slept at Genappe, arrived at Quatre Bras, and consulted Vivian, whose brigade of the 10th and 18th Hussars and the 1st Hussars of the King's German Legion were providing the forward pickets. Vivian told the Duke that, apart from the early morning affair of the outposts, all was quiet and, as yet, the French had shown no signs of movement. A patrol of the 10th Hussars, under Captain

Grey, was sent out, found French cavalry vedettes in possession of the Namur road, and managed to contact the Prussians at Tilly, covering the Prussian retreat from Blücher's reverse at Ligny. By 7.30 a.m. this intelligence was in Wellington's hands, showing that Napoleon had not been able to secure a decisive victory over the Prussians; nor had the French pursuit been vigorous.

Whilst the patrol of the 10th Hussars was away, Wellington received despatches from England. He dealt with them, then lay down at the roadside by the Quatre Bras crossroads and, covering his head with one of the despatch sheets, went to sleep. At 9 a.m. he awoke, and remarked with some astonishment at the inactivity of the French. There then arrived a Prussian officer, Von Massow, sent by General Gneisenau after he had consulted with Marshal Blücher. He informed the Duke of the Prussian concentration at Wavre and asked the Duke's intentions. Wellington told him that if he could be assured of the support of a single Prussian corps he would take up the position at Mont St Jean in front of Waterloo and fight. Without this support, he would have to sacrifice Brussels and withdraw behind the River Scheldt. As Von Massow left for the Prussian headquarters, the Duke commented: 'Old Blücher has had a damned good hiding, and has gone back eighteen miles to Wavre. We must follow his example. I suppose they will say in England that we have been beaten too!' At 10 a.m. Wellington, having decided to withdraw to the position at Waterloo, ordered that the retreat of the infantry was to be covered by all the cavalry and horse artillery and two battalions of light troops. Orders were sent to Lord Hill, commanding the 2nd Corps, to march with the 2nd and 4th Divisions from Nivelles direct to Waterloo.[6]

The infantry divisions of Cooke, Picton and Perponcher came in from the right and left flanks of the Quatre Bras positions, whilst the light infantry continued to maintain the line of outposts, only withdrawing as their supporting infantry retired. Each infantry division halted on the ground vacated by its predecessor, and then fell in to march in turn along the road to Brussels. The rearguard infantry division, Alten's, was able to commence its retreat by 11 a.m., but marched by way of Baisy and the bridge over the River Genappe at Ways le Hutte in order to relieve congestion on the other road. By 11.30 a.m. the last of the infantry had disappeared.

In the meantime the King's Dragoon Guards had been standing by their horses, ready to mount since daylight. At 8 a.m. the regiment was ordered to water the horses a little way to the rear, and it then resumed its position. At noon the cavalry were ordered to take up station on a large plain opposite the French, and by 1 p.m. only they remained in position, with their commander, Lord Uxbridge, seated on a bank by the roadside accompanied by his aide de camp, waiting to see what would happen next.[3,6]

Napoleon, with the main part of the French army, did not set out from the battlefield of Ligny until between 11 a.m. and noon, and reached Marbais by 1 p.m. expecting to hear the sound of battle at Quatre Bras or news from Marshal Ney. Hearing nothing, he decided to march on Quatre Bras himself, and meeting his 1st Cavalry Division under Jacquinot, deployed it to act as his advance guard. Some two miles short of Quatre Bras the scouts of the French 7th Hussars met the British vedettes and fell back before them. The Emperor at once formed his line of battle and halted. He then tried to contact Ney, by sending a detachment of Colonel Marbot's 7th Hussars towards Frasne. They bumped into the Red Lancers of the Guard, who were with Ney, and began to fire at their compatriots thinking them to be English. They then captured an Englishwoman, a camp-follower, who on being questioned by Napoleon revealed that only Lord Uxbridge's cavalry stood to bar his way. Furious that Wellington should have slipped away, the Emperor determined to capture as much of the British cavalry as he could.

The French infantry were ordered to follow D'Erlon's advance corps up the road to Brussels, flanked by Domon's chasseurs and Milhaud's cuirassiers. Meanwhile the Emperor, with an escort of Service squadrons of the Guard and the Horse Artillery of the Guard, galloped to the head of the advance cavalry in order to bring vigour to the pursuit.

Lord Uxbridge, sitting on his bank, was joined by Wellington, who watched the front through his telescope. Suddenly, at about two miles distance, a mass of the enemy were seen, their accoutrements flashing in the sun. At first the Duke thought that they were infantry bayonets, but as they drew closer, they could be seen to be massed squadrons of cuirassiers. Uxbridge pointed out that with defiles in the rear of his cavalry, and with the infantry now too far withdrawn to give effective support, they were not in a good position to withstand the French advance. The Duke agreed and the order was given to retreat in three columns, a centre column and two flank columns.

The centre column was made up of the 1st and 2nd Heavy Brigades, with a rearguard of the 23rd Light Dragoons and the 7th Hussars.[6] The order to retire reached the King's Dragoon Guards at about 2 p.m., where they formed part of the 1st Heavy (Household) Brigade, and as they steadily retired down the Brussels road they halted from time to time and formed up on either side of the road.[3] The French did not attempt to follow the flank columns, but made their main effort against the centre.

The sunshine of the morning had by now given place to a mass of dark clouds and driving wind. Sergeant Major Page remembered how as the French advanced 'there was one of the heaviest storms of rain ever known accompanied by thunder and lightning. The fall of rain was so very heavy that in the fields, which were covered with corn, our horses sunk in every step up to near the hock. It is out of my power herein to express our situation – our boots were filled with water, and as our arms hung down by our sides the water ran off a stream at our finger ends.'[10] Even Captain Naylor remarked that 'we experienced the most severe fall of rain I ever beheld'.[3]

The two heavy brigades had been the first of the British cavalry to retire and they formed the head of the centre column. Having crossed the bridge at Genappe, and the thunderstorm having passed over (although it was still raining heavily), the two brigades rode up the narrow winding street of Genappe. There was not a soul to be seen; the houses were all shuttered, the water cascading from their roofs to rush in a torrent down the gutter in the centre of the road. The only sounds were of the water, and the ring of horses' shoes on the cobbles.

As the road leaves Genappe it climbs steadily for some 700 yards to a ridge. Here Lord Uxbridge halted, and deployed the two heavy brigades. Sir William Ponsonby's 2nd Brigade (the Union) was deployed to the right of the road facing the enemy advance, and the 1st Household Brigade on the left of the road, with its right flank standing on the road.[9] Captain Mercer with his battery of horse artillery describes the scene: 'We suddenly came in sight of the main body of our cavalry drawn up across the chausée in two lines, and extending away far to the right and the left of it. It would have been an imposing spectacle at any time, but just now appeared to me magnificent, and I hailed it with complacency, for here I thought our fox chase must end. "Those superb Life Guards and Blues will soon teach our pursuers a little modesty! Such fellows! – surely nothing can withstand them".'[5]

Eighteen squadrons of French cavalry were now entering Genappe and as their lancers came through the town they halted for some fifteen minutes facing the rearguard of the British cavalry, their flanks protected by the houses of the main street. Those behind could not see that the front ranks had halted, and as they pressed forward, the whole mass of French cavalry became jammed. Lord Uxbridge, seeing their indecision, ordered the 7th Hussars to charge them. This they did with great spirit, but could make little impression on the dense mass. The French now advanced and drove the 7th back, whereupon the 7th rallied and again pushed the French back into the town. The French had by now established a horse battery on the left of Genappe, and the 7th Hussars were losing officers and men. Lord Uxbridge withdrew the 7th from this see-saw contest and they retired through the ranks of the 23rd Light Dragoons and reformed in a field adjoining the road. Uxbridge then ordered the 23rd to advance, but this order was not received with the enthusiasm he expected, so he told them to clear off the road, exclaiming 'The Life Guards shall have this honour.' Two squadrons of the 1st Life Guards led by Major Kelly charged with 'right good will'. The French met the charge with firmness, but were completely overthrown; horses and men were left sprawling in all directions, trampled down and slaughtered. The Life Guards then cleared the main street of Genappe, pushing back the French cavalry.

An eyewitness, Captain Johnnie Kincaid of the 95th Rifles, remarked: 'It did one's heart good to see how cordially the Life Guards went at their work; they had no idea of anything but straightforward fighting, and sent their opponents flying in all directions. The only thing they showed was in everyone who got a roll in the mud (and owing to the slipperiness of the ground there were many), going off to the rear, according to their Hyde Park custom, as being no longer fit to remain on parade!'[12]

The left half-squadron of the King's Dragoon Guards had also been engaged in a sharp conflict with the French advance guard.[1] Sergeant Major Page related in a letter dated 12 January 1816 how he 'took a horse on 17th June with a Frenchman's complete kit of arms, saddle bags etc. on him. He had one of his ears nearly cut off. I gave him to a farrier to take care of for me while I was skirmishing with the French Dragoons, but he lost altogether.'[13] At Genappe as the Life Guards charged in columns of divisions down the road, the King's Dragoon Guards formed up behind them for the same purpose, but the Life Guards were successful, making the French retire, and leaving the King's Dragoon Guards to form the rearguard of the brigade until it reached the position at Mont St Jean.[3] After Genappe the French kept their distance, and although on two or three occasions they made as if to attack, they never pressed forward. So the retreat was conducted at a slow pace, retiring by alternate squadrons and with 'perfect regularity'.

As the head of the centre column crossed the valley and climbed the heights of Mont St Jean, they pushed into the rear of the Brunswick infantry, who had lost all semblance of order in their retreat from Quatre Bras. As soon as the rear companies of Brunswickers heard the sound of the horses' feet, without bothering to look behind them they began to crowd and press on those in front. Then, realising the horses were closing on them, and finding it impossible to crush forward further, they broke into the fields. In order to lighten themselves, arms and packs were thrown away, and many fled in confusion.[6]

At this point Napoleon appeared on the ridge behind, mounted

*1st King's Dragoon Guards passing the Duke of Wellington
while moving back from Quatre Bras to Mont St Jean.*

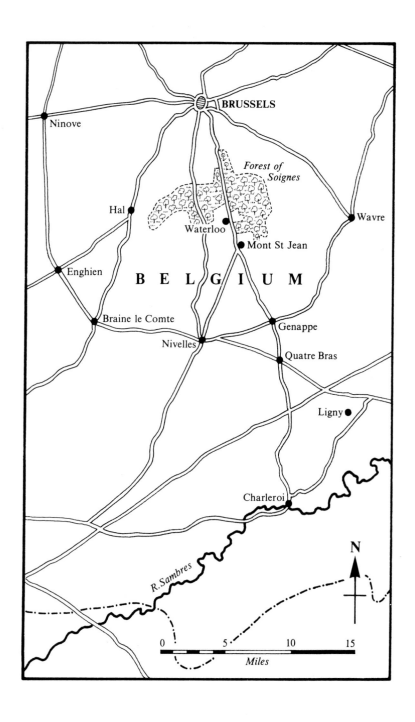

on his white mare, Désirée. His grey dust-coat was soaked, water poured from him; the clasps of his hat had snapped due to the violence of the rain, and its flaps had fallen in front and behind. The Emperor supervised the placing of the guns, as battery after battery accompanying the French advance guard arrived on the scene, and all the time he shouted to the gunner, 'Fire! Fire! These are the English.' But so far as the cavalry were concerned the shot went over their heads and beyond as they climbed the slopes of Mont St Jean.[6]

The centre column wound its way over the ridge, and dropped behind the skyline; then at last the troopers dismounted and bivouacked near the farm of Mont St Jean. Lord Uxbridge summed up the day 'Thus ended the prettiest Field Day of Cavalry and Horse Artillery that I ever witnessed.'[9]

Trumpeter Samuel Wheeler of the King's Dragoon Guards put into verse his feelings about the events of the past two days:

On the 16th June my boys that was the very Day
When we Received Orders for to March Away
To face the tyrants Army My Lads then we was bound
That on the plains of Waterloo Encamped was Around.

We espied our foes Next Morning As in A wood they lay
And like Britons we Advanced to Show them British Play
Our Grape Shot flew Among them to Put them to the Route
But still those Cowardly Raskels Refused to Come Out.

When Wellington Saw their Cowardlyness he Ordered a
    Retreat
Which Order Was Complied With His Design It was Compleat
We Retired through the Village of Geenap As you Soon Shall
    Hear
Followed by A Large Collum of the Enemies Lancers.

But In Our Retreat the Horrid thunder began to Roar
And Rain Like unto Rivuletts upon the Ground did Pour
But our brave English heroes Endured both heat and Cold
And Caused Our foe to Rue the Day the truth I soon unfold.

The first that Charged Was the Lifeguards the Enemy to
  Subdue
They Charged a Collum of the Lancers And Caused them to
  Rue
Till Half An hours hard fighting those heroes Did Endure
And Left 3 hundred Lancers A bleeding in their Gore.

When they Returned from their Work Our Regt. Was Called
  Out
For to face those french Dogs And Put them to the Route
But the Noble Earl of Uxbridge Some Danger Did Espie
Kings Dr Guards threes About he Loudly then Did Cry.

The Cunning french 3 field Pieces had Placed in the town
Thinking As we Advanced to Cut Our heroes Down
But Our brave Commander Soon Ordered us Away –
And then brought up Some English Guns And on them began
  to Play.

Then We Again Retired and Inticed them on the Plain
And Gained a Good Position Wich we was Determined to
  Maintain
But the Night being fast Advancing we Could no Longer see
And Neither of the Armies Could Claim the Victory.[14]

THREE

Waterloo, 18 June 1815

DAYBREAK UNTIL 3 P.M.

The King's Dragoon Guards arrived at Mont St Jean as night fell on 17 June and bivouacked in a patch of arable land, as best they could. The rain eased up as they approached their position, but returned with the darkness and continued all night. Captain Naylor remarked that they bivouacked during incessant rain and without any refreshment or forage.[3] Sergeant Major Page was more explicit: 'We remained in this situation the whole of the night half way up to our knees in mud. Firing commenced the next morning, viz the 18th, at daybreak which made the third day. What seemed worst of all during these three days, we could draw no rations, consequently we were three days without anything to eat or drink.'[10] The horses moved constantly in order to present their backs to the rain and as the men moved around to attend to them and to try to light fires, the whole area soon degenerated into a morass. Some of the men finished what rations remained; some troopers dug up potatoes from a nearby field. Such fires as were lit were made up of wet and green wood, which gave off more smoke than heat. Some of the men huddled together for greater warmth; some slept standing; others remounted and, wrapped in their long cavalry cloaks, tried to sleep bending over their horses' necks; others lay in the mud, and slept the sleep of sheer exhaustion. Perhaps it would have been some comfort to know that the French on the other side of the valley were in no better state.[6]

Before daybreak the men were aroused, and with daylight officers were, for the first time, able to ascertain their position. The pace of the retreat, the closeness of the French pursuit and the constant rain had posed fearful problems for the staff officers, most of whom were inexperienced. As the cavalry arrived they could only point out hastily chosen positions to the brigadiers. These bivouac areas had little to do with battle positions, and were determined by circumstances of arrival rather than any regular or intended disposition.[9] Sergeant Major Page describes how on the morning of the 18th 'we began to get dry, and as the rain ceased we wrung out our clothes, put them on again, and very few of them have been pulled off since'.[10]

Sergeant Major Cotton of the 7th Hussars gave a graphic description of that early morning for the cavalry, after a night of continuous rain. 'The rain descended in torrents, succeeded, as the morning advanced, by a drizzling shower which gradually ceased. Soon after break of day, all who were able were on the move. Many, from cold and fatigue, could not stir for some time; fortunately, on most of us the excitement was too powerful to allow this physical inconvenience to be much felt; although many in after years suffered most severely from it. Some were cleaning arms, others fetching wood, water, straw etc. from Mont St Jean; some trying, from the embers of our bivouac, to light up fires, many of which had been entirely put out by the heavy rain. At this time there was a continual irregular popping along the line, not unlike a skirmish, occasioned by those who were cleaning their fire arms, discharging them, when practicable; which was more expeditious and satisfactory than drawing the charges. Our bivouac had a most unsightly appearance: both officers and men looked blue with cold; and our long beards, with our wet and dirty clothing drying upon us, was anything but comfortable. As morning advanced and all were in motion, one might imagine the whole plain itself to be undergoing a movement. Imagine seventy thousand men huddled together. The buzzing resembled the distant roar of the sea against a rocky coast.'[15]

After daybreak the various regiments of the Household Brigade began to sort themselves out, grooming their horses and cleaning their arms and equipment, and by six o'clock the brigade was assembled in brigade mass on the ground on which they had bivouacked. They were then moved forward a short distance in front of their bivouac area to form the second line and reserve to the infantry who were lying just behind the ridge of Mont St Jean with forward posts at Hougoumont, La Haye Sainte and Papelotte.

The King's Dragoon Guards formed their four squadrons, probably some 530 sabres strong, in the centre of the front rank of the Household Brigade, with two squadrons of the 2nd Life Guards on their left flank, two squadrons of the 1st Life Guards on their right, and the two squadrons of the Blues in reserve. The brigade was stationed on the right-hand side of the main Brussels-Charleroi road, with its left flank touching the road and set back about 200 yards from the crest. The main British position ran along this ridge from Braine l'Alleud to Ohain. The chateau of Hougoumont was about three-quarters of a mile to the brigade's half right front. The farm of La Haye Sainte was some 400 yards directly in front, opposite which was a sandpit garrisoned by three companies of the 95th Rifles. A mile away to the half left were the farms of Papelotte and Smohain. To the rear stood the Forest of Soignies and the brigade's position was some 250 yards in front of the farm of Mont St Jean.

On the other side of the main Brussels-Charleroi road, with its right flank touching the road, was the 2nd Heavy Cavalry Brigade, the Union, made up of the 1st Royal Dragoons, the Scots Greys and the 6th Inniskilling Dragoons. Originally Lord Uxbridge had intended that the various cavalry brigades should be formed into divisions, but due to the circumstances of the retreat they now found themselves dotted along the length of the British line. So throughout the battle small bodies of British cavalry had to face large masses of the French, who concentrated their horse into divisions and corps. Although the British were usually successful at first, the French numbers and concentration often told in the end.

The British cavalry were well mounted. Six weeks of drill and exercise in the Dender valley, with excellent forage, had brought the horses to the peak of condition, although the hard march of the 16th and the retreat of the 17th, with the miserable weather of the preceding night, had inevitably taken its toll. The whole brigade was dismounted with the men being made to lie on the ground beside their horses, so as to avoid the French cannon-fire

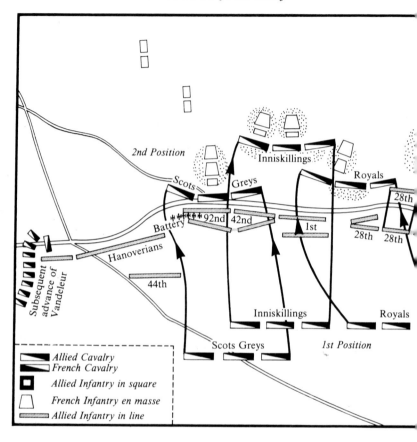

2nd Position

Inniskillings

Scots   Greys   Royals

28th

Battery   92nd   42nd   1st   28th   28th

Hanoverians

44th

Subsequent
advance of
Vandeleur

Inniskillings   Royals

Scots Greys   1st Position

	Allied Cavalry
	French Cavalry
☐	Allied Infantry in square
	French Infantry en masse
	Allied Infantry in line

as much as possible. Lord Edward Somerset detached one
subaltern from each of the four regiments of the brigade, and sent
them to ride forward to the crest of the ridge in order to observe
and report to him on the French movements. To the rear of the
Household Cavalry Brigade were two Dutch-Belgian brigades of
carabiniers and hussars under Van Merle and Trip. In addition,
there were the Hanoverian Cumberland Hussars, who had not
been ordered to dismount and who, as a result, suffered heavily
from the French shells.[6]

Just in front of the Household Brigade, beside the road, there
was a small mud hut, where Sir Andrew Barnard had spent the
night. Some officers of the three companies of the 95th Rifles

30

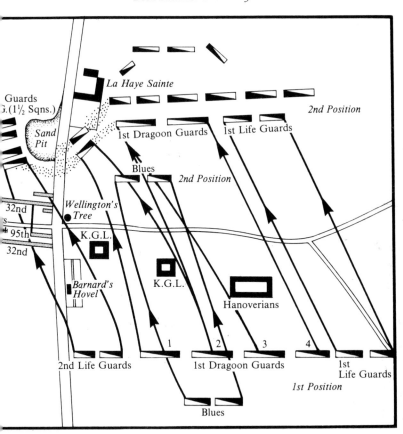

occupying the sandpit to the left of the road had built a fire against the wall of this hovel, on which they boiled a large camp kettle of tea. They generously distributed cups to all who crowded around, only to find that their hospitality left them with none at all themselves.[12]

The British line of battle was formed by 8 a.m. and the Duke of Wellington, dressed in a plain blue frock-coat and mounted on his charger, Copenhagen, inspected the entire position accompanied by Baron Müffling, his Prussian attaché, and a few staff officers. He then returned to the centre of the line to a small tree situated by the crossroads opposite, just above the sandpit and some 200 yards in front of the Household Brigade.

Napoleon intended to start the action by nine o'clock, but his infantry were so far behind and only able to advance up the single Brussels-Charleroi road that it was ten o'clock before the four forward subalterns of the Household Brigade observed thirteen distinct French columns deploying to their positions on the other side of the valley. The Emperor now left the farm of Le Caillou and rode down to La Belle Alliance inn where he spent some time observing the British position. He then rode back as far as Rossomme Farm, dismounted and sat in an armchair by the roadside whilst his infantry marched to their positions. As regiment after regiment passed him, their shouts of 'Vive l'Empereur' drowned the sound of their drums and bugles, and could clearly be heard by the troopers lying beside their horses on the other side of the valley.

By now it was 11 a.m., and the Household Brigade was formed into columns of squadrons behind the infantry and artillery. Captain Naylor noted that 'at twelve a general cannonade commenced, by which we experienced some loss'.[3] 'We lost many men and horses by the cannon of the enemy,' wrote Sergeant Major Page after the battle. 'While covering the infantry we were sometimes dismounted in order to rest our horses, and also when we were in low ground, so that the shot from the French might fly over our heads. Whilst in this situation, I stood leaning with my arm over my mare's neck when a large shot struck a horse by the side of mine, killed him on the spot and knocked me and my mare nearly down, but it did us no injury.'[10] Captain Garland of the 73rd Regiment and Sergeant Major Cotton of the 7th Hussars both noticed that the Household Brigade was kept to the rear of the infantry squares in a bottom or hollow in order to minimise the effect of this shell fire.[9,15]

Napoleon had formed a simple plan of battle. He would start by attacking the farm at Hougoumont on the right flank of the British position in the hope of engaging Wellington's attention and, if possible, drawing the British reserves to the farm. He would then launch his main assault onto the British centre astride the Brussels road, and try to break through there. At 11.15 a.m. Reille, commanding the French 2nd Corps, was ordered to occupy the approaches to Hougoumont. The division of Prince Jerome, Napoleon's brother, on the left flank of Reille's corps, moved into the attack under the cover of the guns of 2nd Corps, which opened fire at 11.35 a.m. Jerome, instead of masking the Hougoumont position by fire and musketry, attempted to storm the post, without success. He persisted in these attacks, which eventually drew in three more French brigades of reinforcements. Hougoumont held, defended by less than two battalions of the Guards.

Napoleon meanwhile was preparing his main assault. He assembled a battery of eighty guns, mostly 12-pounders, opposite the centre of the British position. At 1.30 p.m. three guns of a battery of the Imperial Guards were fired in quick succession as a signal for the 1st French Corps, led by Marshal Ney and D'Erlon, to advance through the battery intervals into the valley below. The French artillery then redoubled its efforts. 'The gunners were standing in line, inserting the charges, ramming them home, swinging the slow matches to make them burn more brightly. They seemed to move as one man. Behind them stood the Captains of the guns; nearly all of them were elderly and they gave their orders as if on parade. Eighty guns fired together, blotting out every other sound. The whole valley was filled with smoke. A second or two later, the calm voices of the Captains could be heard again – "Load – Ram – Aim – Fire". This continued without a break for half an hour. We could scarcely see our comrades, but across the valley the English had also opened fire. We could hear the whistle of their cannon balls in the air, the dull thud as they struck the ground and that other noise when muskets were smashed to firewood, and men hurled twenty paces to the rear, every bone crushed, or when they fell with a limb gone.'[16]

Meanwhile D'Erlon's four divisions, those of Allix, Donzelot, Marcognet and Durutte, altogether 16,000 men strong, marched in divisions from the left, with a gap of 400 yards between the divisions. Each of the first three divisions comprised eight infantry battalions of the line formed in tight columns of closed ranks. Each division had a front of 200 men and was twenty-four deep. Such had been the wastage from years of war that Napoleon could no longer rely on his partially trained recruits to assault in line, so he adopted this mass formation, which had the merit of bringing the full weight of the attack to the crucial point quickly. It also had the disadvantage, as will be seen, of restricting its fire power to the ability of the front rank to load and fire, and it gravely hindered any rapid deployment. The sole exception to this formation was the fourth echelon of Durutte's division, which adopted the traditional French formation of battalions being alternately in line and column. As D'Erlon's divisions descended into the valley, they increased their pace, some men slipping on the greasy ground as they advanced, but their shouts of 'Vive l'Empereur' could be heard above the sound of the cannon.

The Emperor ordered Milhaud to support the attack with Dubois's brigade from Walthers de St Alphonse's 13th Cavalry Division of the 4th Heavy Cavalry Corps. Dubois's regiments, consisting of the 1st and 4th Cuirassiers, moved off at a trot, and bringing up their right shoulders moved across the Brussels road into the land beyond, and then formed brigade line of squadron columns. A hundred yards south of La Haye Sainte the brigade formed into line, galloping through, routing, and almost wiping out in the process a battalion of Hanoverians from Kielmansegge's brigade, which had been sent to reinforce Baring's men of the King's German Legion in the farm of La Haye Sainte. Nine squadrons of cuirassiers came past the farm on the left, and two squadrons on the right, rejoining as they passed to sweep on up the slope towards the centre of the British position to the right of the main road.[6] 'The advance of the enemy's boasted invincible cuirassiers was made with most daring intrepidity, and their appearance was particularly imposing ... Our first line was somewhat shaken, as this immense body of French cuirassiers was advancing to force the centre of the position.'[7]

D'Erlon's infantry advanced on the right flank of the cuirassiers with great gallantry, and Bijlandt's Dutch-Belgian brigade broke and fled before them, having suffered a tremendous pounding and having lost all its senior officers. The remnants of this brigade reformed in the rear of the British position, where it remained for the rest of the day. But this created a gap in the British line, which Picton plugged with Kempt's 8th British Brigade, consisting of the 28th, 32nd Foot and 79th Highlanders. To their left Pack's 9th British Brigade was as hardly pressed, and Pack shouted, 'Ninety-Second, everything has given way on your right and left. You must charge this column.' The whole weight of the attack now fell on Picton's 3rd Division. It seemed as though Dubois's cuirassiers and D'Erlon's infantry were about to break through as they swarmed over the crest of the Mont St Jean ridge. Only 4,000 British infantrymen, albeit all veterans, were there to repel the 16,000 French infantry of the line supported by Dubois's horsemen. Baron Müffling, Wellington's Prussian attaché, noted that the French cavalry, favoured or misled by the thick smoke, penetrated – or accidentally rode into – the space between the British first and second line. Most of the British infantry of Picton's division had been drawn back onto the reverse slope, lying down to escape the cannon fire, and as the French surged over the crest, the redcoats rose to their feet and poured disciplined volley fire into the massed French ranks, who wavered under this hail of musketry. As they rallied and came on again, Picton launched his counter-attack, and as he did so fell dead with a bullet through his head. Again the French seemed to waver.[17]

The four subalterns from the Household Cavalry Brigade who had been posted in the front line to observe the French movements had now reported back to Lord Edward Somerset the advance of the French infantry and cuirassiers. Somerset at once deployed the Household Brigade into line in readiness. Lord Uxbridge had ridden to the right of the British position to supervise the placing of Dornberg and Grant's cavalry brigades. As he returned he observed the French advance, galloped up to Somerset and ordered him to form line and be ready to charge the cuirassiers, keeping the Blues in support. He then crossed the road and ordered Ponsonby to charge D'Erlon's infantry with his Union Brigade the moment he saw the Household Cavalry move, and to hold the Scots Greys in reserve, charging with the Royals and Inniskillings. Uxbridge then returned to the left of the

Household Brigade, taking up position in front of the left-hand squadron, and gave the command to move.[6] Lord Edward Somerset's field trumpeter, John Edwards, sixteen years old, sounded the charge.

Captain Naylor noted that 'we deployed and (I think) about two o'clock a charge was made by the Heavy Brigades through a line of Cuirassiers and a reserve of Lancers'.[3] Sergeant Major Page remembered: 'Our Brigade was mounted, which Brigade is composed of four Regiments – 1st Life Guards, 2nd Life Guards, and Blues four troops each (two squadrons each) and our Regiment eight troops (four squadrons) – our Brigade is commanded by Lord Edward Somerset. At this time the French seemed determined to get possession of a piece of ground where part of our line was drawn up; accordingly they brought forward very heavy columns of infantry and strong bodies of heavy cavalry, and our Brigade was ordered to form line immediately. Now comes the most bloody scene ever known – the French infantry and cavalry came boldly into the bottom of a very large field while we formed at the other end; they charged our infantry and as soon as they showed themselves to our front the word 'charge' was given for our Brigade by Colonel Fuller.'[10]

The Household Cavalry Brigade deployed outwards at 2.20 p.m., moving by threes to left and right, which took the left flank of the brigade across the main Brussels road. The King's Dragoon Guards in the centre and the 1st Life Guards on the right formed line by wheeling threes left, and immediately charged. Due to the crisis to their front there was not time for the whole brigade to get into line before charging, with the result that the 2nd Life Guards were still wheeling by threes to their right after the rest had started to advance.[6]

The King's Dragoon Guards and 1st Life Guards descended into the sunken road athwart the ridge, crossed it, and scrambled up the high bank opposite. Here they checked to steady the line and charged. As they galloped forward, the right flank advanced, so that the 1st and 4th Cuirassiers were struck obliquely. 'The Brigade and the Cuirassiers came to the shock like two walls, in the most perfect lines. I believe this line was maintained

'Cut at the Sword Arm', 1st King's Dragoon Guards.
From Captain James Naylor's sketchbook, 1814.

throughout. A short struggle enabled us to break through them, notwithstanding the great disadvantage arising from our swords, which were full six inches shorter than those of the Cuirassiers, besides it being the custom of our Service to carry the swords in a very bad position whilst charging, the French carrying theirs in a manner much less fatiguing, and also better for either attack or defence. Having once penetrated their line, we rode over everything opposed to us.'[9]

'Left Parry', 1st King's Dragoon Guards.
From Captain James Naylor's sketchbook, 1814.

Uxbridge's charge was timed perfectly, and hit the French at their moment of wavering. The opposing lines met with a crash, and the superior weight of the British heavies, both in men and horses, together with the advantage of the downward slope, overthrew the French, whose horses were blown and winded by their long advance at the trot over slippery ground – much of which was uphill ploughland, into which their horses sank up to their knees.

Johnnie Kincaid recalled how 'the next moment the Cuirassiers were charged by our Household Brigade; and the infantry in our front giving way at the same time, under our terrific shower of musketry, the flying Cuirassiers tumbled in among the routed infantry, followed by the heavies, who were cutting away in all directions. Hundreds of the infantry threw themselves down, and pretended to be dead, while the cavalry galloped over them, and then got up and ran away. I never saw such a scene in all my life.'[12]

Sergeant Major Cotton witnessed the scene. 'Whilst the Cuirassiers were ascending the ridge, our artillery opened with grape and case shot, which laid many low, and disordered their ranks: they however pressed forward most gallantly. Somerset's line was now coming over the ridge, led by Uxbridge, and, at the moment our front squares fired into the Cuirassiers, the two cavalries dashed into each other: the shock was terrific; the swords clashing upon the casques and cuirasses so that, as Lord E. Somerset humorously observed to me – "You might have fancied that it was so many tinkers at work". But it was of short duration. The British Household Cavalry soon cleared the ridge of the cuirassiers, although they made a most gallant resistance: they fled down the slope on both sides of La Haye Sainte, closely followed by the brigade.'[15]

Corporal Stubbings KDG, closely engaged with a cuirassier, narrowly escaped a downward cut from his sabre which took off the ear of his charger. In later years, after his discharge from the army, John Stubbings met his old horse, still serving with the regiment, when a detachment of the King's Dragoon Guards passed through his home village of Market Warsop in Nottinghamshire. 'The meeting between the two was most affecting, the detachment halted in front of the "Hare and Hounds", and villagers turned out to a man to see the "one-eared horse on which John Stubbings rode at Waterloo".'[18]

'We overturned everything, both infantry and cavalry that came in our way, such cutting and hacking never was before seen,' remembered Sergeant Major Page. 'When the French lines broke and ran, our Regiment being too eager, followed the

The charge of the Household Cavalry Brigade at Waterloo.
The officer in the centre thrusting at a Frenchman is a KDG.

French cavalry while the cannon and musketry was sweeping our flank. Many fell and our ranks suffered severely – the Duke of Wellington, with tears, it is said, when he saw us so far advanced among the French, himself said he never saw such a charge, but he was afraid very few of us would return – his words were too true. However, of the 7,000 Frenchmen wearing armour, very few left the field. They were fine men but could not look us in the face, and dreadful was the havoc we made among them.'[10]

Lord Edward Somerset reported: 'Simultaneously with the attack on the left of the high road, information having been received that a large body of the enemy's Cavalry (Cuirassiers and Carabiniers) was moving towards the crest of the position near La Haye Sainte, the 1st Cavalry (Household) Brigade was immediately put in motion (the British Infantry forming squares or columns in order that it might pass through the intervals), and advanced in line (the Blues supporting) to the attack of the enemy's Cavalry, which was met on the ridge of the hill, and was completely defeated and driven back with considerable loss. In the first instance, the 1st Life Guards had a severe conflict with the enemy near La Haye Sainte, where they did great execution, and succeeded in forcing them back to the opposite height, pursuing them to the foot of the French position. The other Regiments of the Brigade were equally successful, and followed that part of the enemy to which they were opposed to a still greater distance.'[9]

In the language of Cannon used twenty-one years after the event, 'those mailed warriors of France were overthrown and pursued with dreadful carnage to the rear of their own lines'.[1]

The 2nd Life Guards on the left of the Household Brigade had been the last regiment to form line, and were galloping towards the sunken road. Some of the French cuirassiers had sought refuge in the deep cutting of the sunken road, and were moving down it. The 2nd Life Guards plunged down on top of them, and they were followed by the left-hand squadron of the King's Dragoon Guards. The French tried to escape, and the whole surging mass of horsemen, cutting and thrusting as they went, poured across the main Brussels road in front of the sandpit. This confused welter of cavalry hit the remains of D'Erlon's infantry, who had just been broken by the Union Brigade charging on the left of the Household Brigade. D'Erlon's terrified infantry were retreating as best they could when into their midst fled the cuirassiers, followed by the 2nd Life Guards and a squadron and a half of the King's Dragoon Guards.

Lieutenant Waymouth of the 2nd Life Guards could not 'determine what portion of the Brigade, nor even of our Regiment, passed to the left of La Haye Sainte, but the circumstances of my more than once, during that advance, finding myself near Major Naylor of the King's Dragoon Guards, and to whom I spoke, leads me to suppose that some part of his Regiment may also have passed to the left. He must have commanded a Squadron, probably the left Squadron of the Kings.'[9]

Later Lieutenant Waymouth managed to see Naylor, who 'distinctly remembers that he commanded the centre squadron of the King's. He remembers that on advancing, Colonel Fuller placed himself by him, and that the first obstacle they encountered was the road which runs along the top of the ridge, that it was too wide to leap, and the banks too deep to be easily passed, and that having crossed it, the next obstacle was the enclosure of the farm of La Haye Sainte. He then made towards his left "along with the current of our men, which was setting that way". He then went down the hill still bearing to his left, till he arrived at an enclosure, a large field in which were Lancers. Turning from them he made his way home again round the left of our line.'[9]

The 2nd Life Guards and part of the King's Dragoon Guards had now joined the Royals, Inniskillings and Greys of the Union Brigade, slaughtering D'Erlon's infantry as they went. 'Intoxicated with slaughter and inciting each other to kill, they pierced and cut down the miserable mass with glee.' With yells of triumph, the British cavalry galloped down the slope, sweeping aside the remains of the French infantry and fugitive cuirassiers. Lord Edward Somerset remembers how 'the 2nd Life Guards, on the left of the Brigade, drove a portion of the Cuirassiers across the chausée to the rear of La Haye Sainte, and down the slope in front of the right of Kempt's Infantry Brigade. Here they were joined by the King's Dragoon Guards, who had crossed the road in front of the farm, and the two Regiments becoming mingled with Ponsonby's Cavalry, lost all regularity in the eagerness of the pursuit.'[9] By now the men were out of hand, excited by the conflict, and paying no attention to shouted orders or trumpet calls; they galloped up the other side of the valley and through the Great Battery of French guns.[6] 'Then we got among the gunners, and we had our revenge. Such slaughtering! We sabred the gunners, lamed the horses, and cut the traces and harness. I can yet hear the Frenchmen crying, "Diable!" when I struck at them, and the long drawn out hiss through their teeth as my sword went home.'[20] Several of the French guns were hurled down the valley to the bottom of the hill, and some troopers rode as far as the French Artillery park, where the drivers, some mere boys, sat crying on their horses in the limbers.[6]

'Many French officers were brought up prisoners; they delivered up their swords to our officers. The enemy upon the opposite heights were similarly employed in taking prisoners and destroying such of our cavalry as had ventured too far. In fact most of Ponsonby's brigade (the Union), with a proportion of the Household Brigade, animated by their first success, pursued their advantage too far; they crossed the valley in disorder, and galloped up to the French position in two's and three's and groups, brandishing their swords in defiance, riding along the ridge, sabring the gunners and rendering about thirty guns useless: the bugles, or trumpets, sounding to rally, were unheeded.'[15]

Martin, a young Swiss officer of D'Erlon's infantry, was knocked over by the British cavalry charge, and was trampled down among the dead and dying. He lay for a time pretending to be dead, and as the charge passed over him, he got to his feet and staggered among the corpses and wounded to climb back to his lines, slipping and stumbling over the mud and stalks of rye. Every now and then British troopers rode past him singly or in groups, and although he expected to be cut down, they seemed to ignore him. He limped past the French guns as the gunners were still being slaughtered, and on off the battlefield until he came to a sunken lane, where he rested and realized for the first time that he had a bayonet wound in his leg, and his foot was hurting from where a horse had trodden on it.[21]

Müffling, the Prussian attaché, related how 'the English cavalry, too eager in its pursuit, was obliged to retreat. Some files, rushing through every obstacle, met a column of the enemy's artillery, consisting of five batteries, which being entirely without escort, necessarily fell into our hands. It being impossible to bring off the guns, they stabbed the horses, and thus rendered the artillery useless during several hours of the battle. It was not till the evening, that the enemy succeeded in making it again moveable by means of reserve horses.'[22]

Uxbridge after the battle thought that more than forty French guns were put out of action by the charge, but none of them could be brought off, as the pursuit had been carried too far, and in too disorderly a manner. In addition, the second line of British cavalry had not followed the heavies, whose horses were now exhausted, and who now had to withstand the attacks of fresh French cavalry. 'After the overthrow of the Cuirassiers I had in vain attemped to stop my people by sounding the Rally, but neither voice nor trumpet availed; so I went back to seek the support of the 2nd Line, which unhappily had not followed the movements of the Heavy Cavalry.'[9]

The main part of the King's Dragoon Guards, two and a half squadrons, continued their charge to the right of the farmhouse buildings of La Haye Sainte along with the 1st Life Guards and the Blues. These farm buildings had acted as a breakwater, and the King's Dragoon Guards, being in the centre of the Household Brigade, swept past on either side and were then separated, one and a half squadrons bearing to the left and two and a half to the right. The two and a half KDG squadrons, together with the 1st Life Guards and Blues, swept all before them as far as the ridge between La Belle Alliance and the south-west of Hougoumont. But here they suffered many casualties from the musketry fire of Bachelu's infantry. The King's Dragoon Guards and 1st Life Guards then rallied behind the Blues, and regained the cover of the main British position. Lord Greenock, Assistant Quarter

Master General of the Cavalry, tells how 'on the right of the Haye Sainte, the Household Brigade, when one of its Regiments – the King's Dragoon Guards – having been likewise too eager in the pursuit, had been almost annihilated, the Life Guards and Blues, having been kept better in hand, had then suffered (comparatively speaking) but little loss.'9

Lieutenant John Hibbert summed up the position: 'Our Brigade, never having been on service before, hardly knew how to act. They knew they were to charge, but never thought about stopping at a proper time, so that after entirely cutting to pieces a large body of Cuirassiers double their number, they still continued to gallop on instead of forming up and getting into line; the consequence was that they got amongst the French infantry and artillery, and were miserably cut up. They saw their mistake too late, and a few, (that is about half the regiment) turned and rode back again.'2

Sergeant Major Cotton saw 'some of Reille's troops who had advanced in support of D'Erlon's attack, fire down from the high banks of the Genappe road upon our men, who had to get back to our line as well they could. Most of the King's Dragoon Guards had dashed over the road and were falling back to reform; but they lost many men and some officers, by the enemy's fire from the little garden of La Haye Sainte.'15

Captain Naylor writes: 'Our attack was almost completely successful, but our men were too sanguine in the pursuit of the fugitive Cuirassiers and at the moment our horses were blown, we were attacked by a multitude of Lancers who did us considerable injury. Our attack was made under a very heavy fire of Artillery and Musketry. It was some time before we could collect our men.'3

Sergeant Major Page relates how 'Colonel Fuller soon fell at our head – deeply regretted. We lost few men by their swords; it was the grapeshot and the musketry that cut us down before we got amongst them. We had to charge to meet them so far over heavy ground that many of our horses were stuck in deep mud. The men were obliged to jump off, leave them, and seek their safety away from the cannon fire.'

'My mare carried me in fine style; she got a light wound in her off hind leg by a French Lancer. I was after a French Officer who was riding away from me. I came up to him and he thrust his lance at me, I turned it with my sword, it glanced down and cut my mare below the hock of the off hind leg. I was struck by a musket shot on the left thigh, but it was prevented from doing me any harm in a singular manner, which was a follows. The day before my sabre tasche, which is a kind of pocket made of leather, had one of the carriages broken, and in order to keep it safe it was taken up very short and lodged on my left thigh. The pocket being very full of books and other things prevented the shot from going right through when it struck me. This shot would have fractured my thigh-bone had not the sabre tasche prevented it.'[10]

Captain Robert Wallace KDG wrote that 'as far as my recollection goes, we were more in contact with the French Heavy Cavalry, than with other troops, and many, I am sure, suffered severely from the men of the 1st Dragoon Guards, as did ours also from them, many of our men having severe sabre wounds, particularly about the face.'[23]

Those of the King's Dragoon Guards who had gone to the left of La Haye Sainte now found themselves scattered and mixed with the remnants of the Union Brigade, their horses blown, in the midst of the French position. 'The enemy fled as a flock of sheep across the valley, quite at our mercy. In fact our men were out of hand. The General, his staff and every officer within hearing exerted themselves to the utmost to reform the men; but the helplessness of the enemy offered too great a temptation to the dragoons, and our efforts were abortive. It was evident that the enemy's reserves of cavalry would soon take advantage of our disorder. If we could have formed a hundred men we could have made a respectable retreat, and saved many; but we could effect no formation, and were as helpless against their attack as their infantry had been against ours. Everyone saw what must happen. Those whose horses were best, or least blown, got away.'[9]

Napoleon now brought up the Gobrecht Brigade of Jacquinot's Division, consisting of the 3rd and 4th Lancers under Colonel Bro and Colonel Martigne, who spread from the left by

An attack by the King's Dragoon Guards at Waterloo.
The regiment engaging French cuirassiers.

Papelotte and chased any British cavalryman they could see, also lunging with their lances at any wounded lying on the ground. From the French centre above La Belle Alliance came two regiments of cuirassiers, the 5th and 10th under General Delort from Milhaud's 4th Cavalry Corps, and they began to sweep the valley in pursuit of the Household Brigade.[16,24] 'No sooner had they got about five hundred yards from the French infantry [wrote John Hibbert] than they were met by an immense body of Lancers who were sent for the purpose of attacking them in this way. Our men were rendered desperate by their situation. They were resolved either to get out of the scrape or die, rather than be taken prisoners, so they attacked them, and three troops cut their way through them; about a troop were killed or taken prisoner.'[2]

Uxbridge, in personally leading the charge of the two heavy cavalry brigades, showed great bravery, but he also lost control. 'This forces from me the remark', he later said, 'that I committed a great mistake in having myself led the attack. The carrière once begun, the leader is no better than any other man; whereas if I had placed myself at the head of the 2nd line, there is no saying what great advantages might not have accrued from it . . . Had I, when I sounded the Rally, found only four well-formed Squadrons coming steadily along at an easy trot, I feel certain that the loss the first line suffered when they were finally forced back would have been avoided, and most of the guns might have been secured, for it was obvious the effect of that charge had been prodigious, and for the rest of the day, although the Cuirassiers frequently attempted to break into our lines, they always did it "mollement", and as if they expected something more behind the curtain.'[9]

But the second line was not in support, and there was no one to order them forward, with Uxbridge in front of the first line. Waymouth said, 'I often heard Uxbridge blamed for having thrown away our Brigade by making it charge without an adequate support. When we were all lying on the ground in order to avoid as much as possible the effect of the Enemy's cannonade, I saw a certain Hanoverian Regiment, which we knew as "The Duke of Cumberland's Hussars", in line in our rear. My thoughts at the time were what could possess them to sit upon their horses to be knocked over by cannon balls when they saw our Brigade upon the ground. I always have understood that this Regiment was ordered to charge in our support, but that when we attacked they ran away.'[9] Lord Uxbridge himself commented, 'I have the strongest reason to be excessively dissatisfied with the General commanding a Brigade of Dutch Heavy Cavalry, and with a Colonel commanding a young Regiment of Hanoverian Hussars.'[9]

At length the 12th and 16th Light Dragoons of Vandeleur's Brigade came forward. Vandeleur in the absence of Uxbridge, acting at last on his own initiative, wheeled the 12th and 16th into line, and ordered the 11th Light Dragoons to support him. They charged from the left of the British line right-handed into the valley. They crashed through Durutte's division and attacked the French lancers. They, in turn, suffered from the fire of Durutte's division, as had the Household Brigade. Durutte's division was the one French division of D'Erlon's corps which did not advance in mass, and which was able to retain its cohesion and manoeuvrability, aided by its being on the right of the French advance. Merle's Dutch-Belgian Brigade and Vivian's Light Cavalry Brigade also moved to support, but arrived too late to be of use. Vivian saw 'Lord Edward Somerset with the wretched remains of the two Heavy Brigades, not 200 men and horses, retire through me'.

Even in the chaos and tragedy of the withdrawal, regimental spirit prevailed. Captain Clark-Kennedy of the Royals saw a small party of the King's Dragoon Guards that had joined in the charge on the left-hand side of the Brussels road; they were retiring on the left of his squadron. Mistaking them for some of his own men – for the uniform of the King's Dragoon Guards and the Royals was very similar – he called out to them, 'Royals, form on me.' The reply came, 'We are King's Dragoon Guards – not Royals'; and they rode on.

As the two and a half KDG squadrons, together with the 1st Life Guards and Blues, reformed on their original position, the stragglers dribbled in from the remains of the squadron and a half

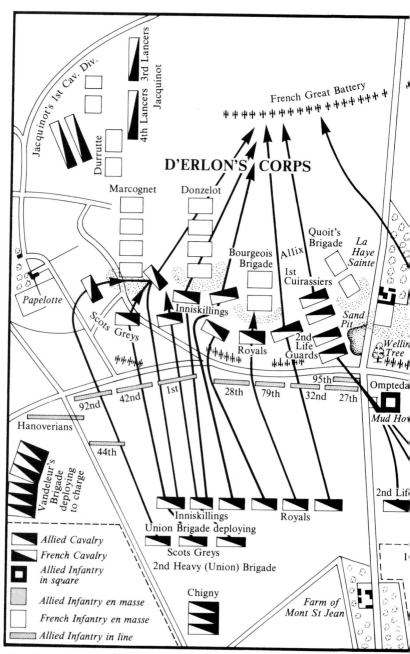

Situation at 2.30 p.m.

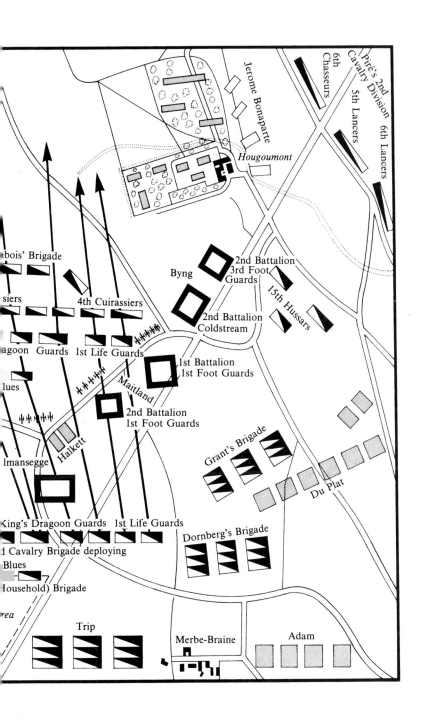

Piré's 2nd
Cavalry Division 6th Lancers

6th
Chasseurs

5th Lancers

Jerome Bonaparte

Hougoumont

bois' Brigade

siers

4th Cuirassiers

2nd Battalion
3rd Foot
Guards

Byng

15th Hussars

agoon Guards   1st Life Guards

2nd Battalion
Coldstream

lues

Maitland

1st Battalion
1st Foot Guards

Imansegge

2nd Battalion
1st Foot Guards

Halkett

Grant's Brigade

King's Dragoon Guards   1st Life Guards

Du Plat

Cavalry Brigade deploying

Dornberg's Brigade

Blues

Household) Brigade

rea

Trip

Merbe-Braine

Adam

English and French Dragoons.
The left sleeve cuff of the English Dragoon shows him
to be a 1st Royal Dragoon, the right to be a KDG!
Note the reins held in the teeth
in order to free the left hand.

that had charged to the left of La Haye Sainte. Naylor tells us that
'Turner with about thirty men joined the Brigade'.[3] As the
remains of the Household Brigade reformed, it was joined by
what was left of the 2nd Heavy (Union) Cavalry Brigade. It had
been a brilliant charge, perfectly timed to achieve the maximum
effect, but then marred by the lack of discipline and over-
eagerness so often displayed by the British cavalry. John Hibbert
has the last word: 'However it had this good effect – that the
astonishing bravery displayed by the Heavy Brigade entirely
appalled the French.'[2]

The verses of Trumpeter Samuel Wheeler describe this part of
the action:

Then we Lay by for the Night With our horses by Our Sides
To tell the Sufferings we Endured No Pen Can Never Describe
For the Rain Descended In torrents the Lightening flashed so
    blue
Still each Briton kept his Spirits up his foes to Subdue.

Then Early the Next Morning Our Out Piquets did Espye
Napoleon And his Army that was Advancing Nigh
Our Army being Ready the Cannon began to Roar
And Muskett Shot Into their Lines So Quickly we did Pour.

About ten O'Clock In the forenoon In A body Our Cavalry
    Lay
Their Shots and Shells Into Our Collum So briskly they did
    play
Two heavy Brigades then formed A line In Readiness to
    Advance
To Charge the tyrants Curisears Wich was the Pride of France.

Lord Somerset Commanded the Household Brigade
And Led us On to victory through the hottest of Cannonade
So well the Brigade then Played their Parts And Charged them
    so free
Wich was the Cause my british boys of Gaining the Victory.

O When we Came up With them the Slaughter It was Great
Our Gallant troops So boldly had Soon Caused their lines to
    Break
We charged them So boldly And Made them far to Run
And Cut them down With Our broad swords Like Motes In
    the Sun.

General Ponsonby's brigade Charged Next And I Am bound to
    Say
They Done ther Duty Manfully upon that Glorious Day
They Charged them So valiantly And Caused them to Rue
That Ever they fought for boneypart on the Plains of
    Waterloo.[14]

FOUR

Waterloo, 18 June 1815

3 P.M. TO NIGHTFALL

As the remains of the Household Cavalry Brigade returned and reformed in its old position some 200 yards behind the crest of the main slope of Mont St Jean, survivors trickled in, some in small parties, some in ones and twos. It was at once clear just how severe the casualties had been. Lord Edward Somerset noted that the 2nd Life Guards and one and half squadrons of the King's Dragoon Guards who had charged to the left of La Haye Sainte had 'encountered a heavy fire, and sustained a very severe loss in their retreat. Colonel Fuller, commanding the 1st Dragoon Guards, and several Officers and men of that Regiment fell in this attack.'[9] John Hibbert commented, 'Poor Colonel Fuller and Major Graham are killed, I am afraid, without doubt, although they are returned missing.'[2]

There is some confusion over where Colonel William Fuller died. Lord Edward Somerset, commanding the brigade, thought that 'Colonel Fuller must, on arriving at the farm of La Haye Sainte, have turned to his right, for I believe there is no doubt of his having been killed down the slope of our position, to the right of La Haye Sainte'.[9] Another account says that the Colonel was killed at the south-west corner of the orchard of the farm La Haye Sainte 'while gallantly leading the centre squadron' of the King's Dragoon Guards.[6] A description of the charge written just after the battle stated that 'Colonel Fuller of 1st Dragoon Guards as also Major Graham and Cornet the Hon. H. B. Bernard and another officer were taken prisoners; for a long time their friends hoped they would return but though the particulars of their fate remain uncertain there can be no doubt that they were "murdered by the enemy like many other brave unfortunate men".'[24] Yet another account states that 'Colonel Fuller was killed whilst pursuing the Cuirassiers: he boldly led his Regiment up the French height on the allied left of the Charleroi road.'[25] And a fifth version describes how 'many officers met their death in striving to rally their soldiers, and like the Colonels of the Scots Greys and the King's Dragoon Guards were slain within the French position'.[25]

Lieutenant Colonel William Fuller

John Hibbert gives a sixth account: 'In this affair poor Fuller lost his life; His horse was killed by a lance, and the last time he was seen he was unhurt but dismounted. Of course the Lancers overtook him and killed him, for our men were on the full retreat; he made a sad mistake pursuing the Cuirassiers so far.'[2] There is no doubt that William Fuller died, killed in action, but how or where remains shrouded in the excitement of the charge and in the fog of battle. Each description, however, typifies a way in which individual King's Dragoon Guards did die in that charge.

Major Henry Graham, 1st King's Dragoon Guards.
He is depicted wearing staff officer's uniform,
but he returned to regimental duty in 1815.

Major Henry Graham, who also was killed, had been a major since 1811; Cornet Bernard, the fifth son of Viscount Brandon, was only eighteen years old and had been commissioned for a year and three days. They were not the only officer casualties. Major John Bringhurst, who had served with the King's Dragoon Guards since 1806, was dead, as was the Adjutant, Lieutenant Tom Shelver, along with Captain Battersby and Lieutenant Brook. John Hibbert records: 'You may conceive what a slaughter it was when we lost five entire troops out of eight.'² The numbers lost in the charge, not only of dead, but of those missing and wounded, together with the casualties among the horses, reduced the King's Dragoon Guards to three effective troops.

'It was some time before we could collect our men,' remembers James Naylor. 'Captain Turner, with about thirty men, joined the Brigade; he was wounded soon after by a cannon shot in the arm and I took the command of the K.D.G.'s.'³ While the regiment reformed and took stock there was a lull in the battle. Wellington moved his infantry back again behind the ridge of Mont St Jean and ordered them to lie down for shelter from the artillery fire. The cavalry were not so fortunate; having been rallied and formed nearly on their original post, they had to continue mounted in support of the infantry.⁹ Most of the movement on the British side at this period seemed to be backwards and to the rear, as the wounded and masses of prisoners were escorted towards Brussels.²⁶ The farriers of the King's Dragoon Guards were used for this duty. The time was now about 3.30 p.m.

Marshal Ney was ordered by Napoleon to renew the attack on La Haye Sainte. The fire from the French Great Battery increased in tempo, with Napoleon also bringing into action the hiterhto uncommitted batteries of the Imperial Guard. General Alten, commanding the 3rd Anglo-Hanoverian Infantry Division, thought that 'never had the oldest soldiers heard such a cannonade'. Ney, misled by the smoke, the fact that the British infantry had retired behind the crest and laid down, and the drift to the British rear of prisoners and wounded (which the French mistook for signs of retreat), thought that a massive cavalry charge against the British centre on the ridge would provide the *coup de grâce* and drive the Allied army from the field. Ney at once despatched his staff to summon the brigade and divisional commanders of the massed French cavalry. Having gathered eight regiments of cuirassiers, together with the lancers and chasseurs of the Imperial Guard, he himself led these forty-three squadrons of magnificent cavalry against the centre of the British position. On their right, close to La Haye Sainte, were the cuirassiers; then the lancers, and *chasseurs à cheval* of the

Major John D. Bringhurst, 1st King's Dragoon Guards.
Killed in action at Waterloo.

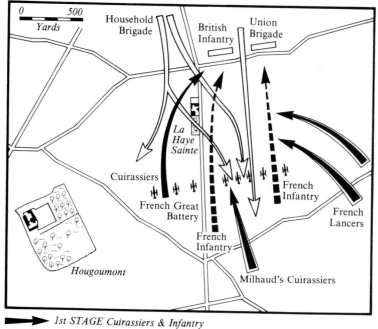

0 — 500
Yards

Household Brigade
British Infantry
Union Brigade
La Haye Sainte
Cuirassiers
French Great Battery
French Infantry
Hougoumont
French Infantry
French Lancers
Milhaud's Cuirassiers

▶ 1st STAGE Cuirassiers & Infantry
▷ 2nd STAGE British Cavalry charge
▶ 3rd STAGE French Lancers & Milhaud's Cuirassiers counter charge

Imperial Guard. They advanced in lines, in echelon, their left reaching nearly to the east hedge of Hougoumont.[15]

'As those on the right neared the ridge, the French artillery discontinued firing; and ours opened with grape, canister and shrapnel shells, which rattled like hail on the steel-clad warriors; but they still pressed on, regardless of our fire, towards the British guns, the horses of which had been sent to the rear. Every discharge (the load was usually double), threw them into great disorder; but excited by the trumpets sounding the charge, they rode up to the cannons' mouths, shouting "Vive l'Empereur".

'Our gunners fled to the squares, which were all ranged in chequer; the front ones had advanced again nearly close to the guns. The French, not perceiving the advantage which the squares afforded the gunners, and imagining that they had captured the guns, shouted out in triumph, and then crossed over the ridge; here they were assailed by a rolling fire from our squares, which were all prepared, the front ranks on the right knee, the next rank at the charge.

'When the cuirassiers had passed over the ridge, they were out of sight of the lancers and chasseurs, who immediately pressed on to share in the contest. Our artillery received them in like manner; some of the artillery men rushing back to their guns, and after discharging them at the foe, taking shelter again within the squares, or under the guns. The firing produced a much greater effect upon such of the enemy's cavalry as were not protected by the cuirass and casque; consequently their ranks were much more disordered than were the cuirassiers; still they pursued their onward course, passed the guns, raised a shout and swept round the squares. Some halted and fired their pistols at the officers in the squares; others would ride close up, and either cut at the bayonet or try to lance the outside files. No sooner had the broken squadrons passed the guns, than the gunners were again at their post, and the grape rattled upon the retiring hosts; but frequently, before a succeeding round could be discharged, the hostile cavalry were again upon them, and compelled them to seek shelter.

'During the French cavalry attacks, they were at one time riding about amidst our squares for three quarters of an hour; all cannonading having ceased between the two high-roads.'[15]

The 1st Heavy (Household) Cavalry Brigade, or what remained of it, was drawn up on its original position of that morning, and as the waves of French cavalry came surging through the British squares of infantry Lord Uxbridge placed himself at the head of one squadron and gave the order to charge again. The heavy cavalry fell on the advancing cuirassiers, lancers and chasseurs and went for them hammer and tongs. The time was now 4.15 p.m. The enemy suffered severely; their horses were blown and they were at the end of their charge, whereas the King's Dragoon Guards, Life Guards and Blues were at the start of theirs. But the French fought bravely in a spirited cavalry hand-to-hand contest, where both horsemanship and skill at arms decided the difference between death and survival. One slashing back-hand stroke severed a cuirassier's head and helmet and sent it flying some distance. His horse galloped on, in obedience to the reins, with the headless rider sitting erect for a while in his saddle until finally toppling to the ground. 'We galloped at the cuirassiers and fairly rode them down; when they were unhorsed, we cracked them like lobsters in their shells, and by the coming up of the cannon afterwards, many of them were squeezed flat as pancakes.'[9] Captain Wallace remembered how most of the King's Dragoon Guards slashed at all and sundry, including those of the enemy lying on the ground. Wallace, in passing a dismounted French trumpeter lying on the ground, spared him as he galloped past. 'I did not slash at him but the trumpeter slashed at me!' The Brigade suffered more casualties in this second charge; Colonel Ferrier of the Life Guards and Major Packe of the Blues were killed, along with several other officers and men.[9]

There then developed a see-saw of charges. In all, the ever-diminishing numbers of the Household Brigade charged eleven or twelve times, being now kept well in hand, and darting forward at the appropriate moment each time. During these repeated charges many men were being killed or severely wounded, and their horses, having lost their riders, tried to stay with the squadrons. As the ranks formed for a new charge, so these riderless mounts formed up alongside the mounted men and joined in the charge. Even when they were wounded, they kept up in formation, just so long as they had the strength to gallop. Other horses too badly hurt to move still fed on the grass within their reach as they lay on the ground.[27]

By now the French cavalry attack was losing its impetus. Lord Uxbridge remembered that although the French 'frequently attacked our squares', it was 'never in overwhelming masses, and with that vigour and speed which would have given them some chance of penetrating. It was chiefly made and frequently repeated by masses of Cuirassiers, but never in one connected line, and after the first grand attack of the morning they never came on with the degree of vigour which could give them a hope of penetrating into our immovable Squares of Infantry.'[9]

Sergeant Major Cotton described how 'at one time that memorable afternoon, the ridge and rear slope of our position were literally covered with every description of horsemen, lancers, cuirassiers, carabiniers, horse-grenadiers, light and heavy dragoons and hussars. The menacing approach of the French cavalry, who rode amongst and around our squares, was not quietly witnessed by our own horsemen: we made many spirited charges between and on every side of the allied squares. When at length the enemy's gallant but fruitless efforts became exhausted, our cavalry appeared and cleared the allied position.'[15]

After a particularly heavy cannonade the French sent forward a swarm of tirailleurs, supported by cuirassiers, near La Haye Sainte. The battalion of Hanoverian infantry, mistaking the cuirassiers for British cavalry, did not form square in time and were cut to pieces. At the same time, under cover of this attack, the French established a battery of guns well forward which menaced the centre of the British position. Part of the King's Dragoon Guards and the Blues were moved towards this point, supported by the Hanoverian Cumberland Hussars. The Cumberland Hussars, alarmed by some musketry and a few cannon balls, began to give way. Lord Uxbridge at once sent Captain Williams, his aide-de-camp, to bring them back, but without success. Uxbridge then sent Captain Seymour, who took the Colonel of the Cumberland Hussars by the collar and nearly shook him out of the saddle. After appealing to the next in command, to no avail, he seized the bridle of Colonel Hake's horse to lead him forcibly back to his post, in the hope that his men would follow. But the entire regiment fled, and on reaching Brussels spread false alarms about the progress of the battle. As a result the Colonel was later cashiered and the regiment disbanded.[15]

Lord Edward Somerset then led the remaining King's Dragoon Guards and Blues down to meet the French attack, but they were too few in numbers to do more than check the movement. Uxbridge then rode up to Trip's Dutch Belgian Heavy Cavalry Brigade, addressed them and turned to lead them into action. He crossed the ridge of Mont St Jean, and started on the descent, when he realised that he was on his own. He at once returned to Trip and expressed his feelings in no mean fashion.[15] But the French had now stormed and captured La Haye Sainte and were holding it firmly.

It was now 5.30 p.m., and the tattered remains of the Household Cavalry Brigade reformed in its original position. Not for long however, as Uxbridge again sent for it to move to the right of the British position in order to counter a new threat posed by a formidable column of French infantry advancing to the attack, suported by cavalry. The brigade formed and charged this new menace. As it galloped down onto the head of the French column, it was met by a heavy fire of musketry, which emptied many saddles. Again it succeeded in stopping the advance and it inflicted immense loss on the infantry, but by now it was too weak in numbers to succeed in penetrating the column or scattering it.[9]

Yet again the remains of the Household Brigade reformed in their original position. At this point Colonel Edward Lygon, commanding the 2nd Life Guards, had his horse wounded. He left the field, and command of the Household Brigade, under Lord Edward Somerset, devolved upon young Captain James Naylor of the King's Dragoon Guards as the next senior officer. By this time it was a sadly depleted command consisting of only a total of a hundred men of all four regiments – 1st and 2nd Life Guards, Blues and King's Dragoon Guards.[3]

The other British heavy cavalry brigade, the Union, had suffered as badly, and it was now brought across from its position on the left-hand side of the Brussels-Charleroi road to join the Household Brigade on the right-hand side. The Union Brigade, in turn, mustered only the strength of one squadron. So these two composite squadrons, all that remained of seven fine cavalry regiments, were extended into line behind the equally battered remains of the infantry. They received a slight reinforcement in the form of a squadron of the 23rd Light Dragoons, under command of Major Lautur, which had been separated from the rest of its regiment and was attached as welcome extra strength to the now composite Household and Union Brigade.[9]

Lord Uxbridge, seeing the diminished strength of the brigade, advised Lord Edward Somerset to withdraw. But a considerable space on the right of La Haye Sainte was by now without any British infantry; it was covered by Baron Ompteda's Hanoverian infantry, who were showing signs of great unsteadiness. The Hanoverians were supported by the Dutch-Belgian cavalry, but as Lord Edward Somerset remarked to Lord Uxbridge, if the Household troops were to move off, there would be no holding the others.[6,9]

So the composite brigade was extended into a single line in order to make as great a show of force as possible, and there they sat sticking it out, and occupying the gap in the British line. It was now 6.30 p.m. They were constantly exposed to a most destructive fire of both musketry and artillery, and more and more saddles were emptied and horses killed.[9] At about seven o'clock Captain James Naylor, in command of the brigade under Somerset, was himself wounded and forced to leave the field. He was taken to Brussels, where the KDG Regimental Surgeon, William McAuley, attended his wound.[3]

By this time Zieten's Prussian corps, the advance guard of Blücher's army, was starting to arrive on the left flank of the British position. They came onto the field in ever-increasing numbers, exerting more and more pressure as their comparatively fresh troops attacked the French right flank. So Wellington was, at last, able to move troops from his left to the terribly weakened centre. The two light cavalry brigades of Vandeleur and Vivian were brought across to the centre and posted, Vandeleur behind Chassé's Dutch-Belgian division, and Vivian behind the Hanoverians of Kielmansegge. This line of British cavalry prevented both corps of badly shaken troops from leaving the field, and gave heart to the remnants of the British infantry.[6]

As these two brigades of light cavalry crossed the front in columns of troops they passed the single rank of the combined Household and Union Heavy Brigade. Vivian shouted to Somerset, 'Lord Edward, where is your brigade?' 'Here,' said Lord Edward. Vivian describes how 'Somerset pointed to the ground which was strewn with wounded, over whom it was hardly possible sometimes to avoid swerving. Wounded or mutilated horses wandered or turned in circles. The noise was deafening, and the air of ruin and desolation that prevailed wherever the eye could reach gave no inspiration of victory.'[9]

Vivian went on: 'Lord Edward Somerset with the wretched remains of the two Heavy Brigades, not 200 men and horses, retired through me, and I then remained for about half an hour exposed to the most dreadful fire of shot, shell and musketry that it is possible to imagine. No words can give any idea of it (how a man escaped is to me a miracle), we every instant expecting to see the Enemy appearing under our noses, for the smoke was literally so thick that we could not see ten yards off.'[9] It was this barrage of shot and shell that had reduced the combined Household and Union Brigade to a mere hundred men and horses.

Captain Kincaid said that 'the smoke still hung so thick about us that we could see nothing. I walked a little way to each flank, to endeavour to get a glimpse of what was going on; but nothing met my eye except the mangled remains of men and horses, and I was obliged to return to my post as wise as I went. I had never yet heard of a battle in which everybody was killed; but this seems likely to be an exception, as all were going by turns.'[12]

Corporal Stubbings was now Sergeant Stubbings – promoted on the field. He wrote to his father and mother after the battle: 'I take the first opportunity that lays in my Power of informing you that I ham in Good Helth after the very sharp Ingagement Which tooke place on 18th June and Dear father it is a wonder that I escaped without receiving any injury for Whee was very much Exposed to Danger both on 17th and 18th of June and a Most dreadfule Battle indeed and Ham sorry to say our Regiment Suffered severely in Killed and wounded. But thanks be to God that Spared My Life I came out of the field unhurt and I was in the hotest part of it and I Gained Great Praise for My Good and Coregous Beaver in the field and in Consequence of which I Ham Maid Sergeant. It is Dredfule to relate the seens I saw on the 18th. The field for Miles around was covered with the wounded and Slain and in some places My Horse Could Not Pass Without Trampling on them and I am Sorry to inform you that Charles

Stanley fell on that Ever Memorable Day the 18th June fiting Manfully in the Defence of his Country.'[18]

Meanwhile, away on the British right centre Napoleon's last reserve, the Imperial Guard, had attacked the ridge with all the confidence and dash that their years of constant victory had given them. The first column of four battalions of the Middle Guard were thrown back by the disciplined volleys and the charge of Maitland's 1st Brigade of Foot Guards. The second column of four more battalions of the Middle Guard were caught in enfilade by Sir John Colborne's quick thinking and mastery of the 52nd Foot, which he commanded. The 71st and 95th Foot, the other regiments of Adam's brigade, quickly supported them. At the same time the 1st Foot opened fire on the head of the column, and that was enough. The Guard did not wait for the bayonet charge which Colborne had launched, but broke and fled. For the first time the cry was heard – 'La Garde recule!' On the left flank the Young Guard under Duhesme, supported by two battalions of the Old Guard under Morand, strove to keep back the growing Prussian pressure of Bulow's corps at Planchenoit.[6,24,26]

Wellington now ordered the general advance. At this point Uxbridge advised caution and suggested that the troops should not go beyond the opposite heights. Wellington's response was, 'Oh, damn it! In for a penny, in for a pound, is my maxim; and if the troops advance they shall go as far as they can.' The combined Household and Union Brigades, now only numbering a hundred effective men, joined in at once in spite of their lack of numbers. They were stationed in line some 300 yards below the crest of the ridge of Mont St Jean, and about the same distance from the right of the main Brussels-Charleroi road. As the whole British line advanced, the infantry discharging a last volley at the retreating French, the remains of the Household Brigade joined in a final charge. The French were by now a confused mass of cuirassiers, lancers, carabiniers, infantry and artillery, all trying to escape to the rear, whilst the few KDG survivors of that terrible day rode among them cutting and slaughtering all in reach. A panic seized the enemy and they fled on all sides, deserting their artillery, throwing down their arms, each man thinking of his own preservation. Wellington and Uxbridge rode down the slope encouraging all in sight to press the enemy and not give them a chance to stand, when one of the last cannon shots of the day skimmed the neck of Copenhagen, the Duke's horse, and hit Uxbridge in the knee. 'By God,' Uxbridge cried, 'I've lost my leg!' 'By God,' exclaimed Wellington, 'so you have!' Wellington supported him in the saddle until his aide-de-camp and some soldiers dismounted and carried him off.[24,26,28]

The Prussians now took up the pursuit and the Household Brigade halted on the ridge of La Belle Alliance, and the hundred survivors of the Household and Union Brigades bivouacked for the night on the spot where the Old Guard had made its last stand, marked today by their monument of the 'Dying Eagle'. The troopers built camp fires from the debris of the battlefield – broken muskets, lances and bits of cannon wheels and waggons. They sat around warming themselves and trying to cook some dirty lumps of fat they had picked up, using the cuirasses of dead French cavalrymen in which to heat them.[6] In memory of that evening at Waterloo, the officers and sergeants of the King's Dragoon Guards, and now the 1st The Queen's Dragoon Guards, still dine together in the Sergeants' Mess.

Müffling summed up the qualities of the British soldier that day: 'There is not perhaps in Europe an army equal to the British, that is to say, none whose tuition, discipline, and whole military tendency is so purely and exclusively calculated for giving battle. The British soldier is vigorous, well fed, by nature highly brave and intrepid, trained to the most rigorous discipline, and admirably well armed. The infantry resist the attacks of the cavalry with great confidence, and when taken in the flank or rear, British troops are less disconcerted than any other European army. These circumstances in their favour well explain how this army, since the Duke of Wellington conducted it, has never yet been defeated in the open field.'[22]

John Hibbert wrote home: 'Altogether it was a most wonderful victory. No men but the English could have fought better than the French; they left two hundred and twenty pieces of cannon on the field.'[12] And Sergeant Stubbings wrote to his father: 'French killed

The King's Dragoon Guards and French Dragoons at Waterloo.
The officer is wearing breeches and jackboots;
the troopers wear overalls.

and wounded (and prisoner) on 18th June, 85,000 Men and the Duke of Wellington took from them 150 pieces of cannon. Martial Blucher tooke 60 Pices of Cannon and the french fled in all Directions those few that was left.'[18]

But the cost to the King's Dragoon Guards had been frightful. The official Casualty List immediately after the battle gave three officers killed and four missing (although all four proved to be dead), with four officers wounded. The killed were Colonel Fuller, Majors Graham and Bringhurst, Captain Battersby, Lieutenant Brooke, Cornet the Honourable H. B. Bernard, and Adjutant Shelver. The wounded were Captains Turner, Naylor and Sweeney and Lieutenant Irvine. Forty rank and file had been killed and one hundred and twenty-four were still missing (most of whom were later found to be dead), and a hundred had been wounded. Total casualties were reported as 275 out of the 530 who paraded that morning.

It is very difficult to ascertain accurately the exact numbers present in each regiment of the Household Cavalry Brigade. Fortescue in his *History of the British Army* gives 29 KDG officers and 568 other ranks; Dwelley's Muster Roll of other ranks gives 579; Dalton's Waterloo Roll quotes 29 officers, giving a total of 608. Sir Morgan Crofton claims that there were 530 all ranks; George Jones's *Battle of Waterloo*, published by James Booth in 1817, gives the number of KDG all ranks as 529, whereas Siborne gives 530. The Mint Medal Roll gives the total of Waterloo Medals issued to the regiment as 577. To this figure must be added a further 31 names of officers and men who were killed, and whose relatives apparently did not apply for a medal. This would give a grand total of 608 officers and men in Belgium which agrees with Dalton's Roll. The Official Returns of the Strength and Losses state that the regiment paraded 571 all ranks on 18 June. But this figure would include the rear party and farriers (who were ordered to tend the wounded) and any sick; so the figure of about 530 all ranks present with the regiment at Waterloo seems a reasonable assumption to make from the mass of conflicting evidence.

The final count of casualties made days later showed seven

officers killed and four wounded. Two sergeant majors, eleven sergeants and 109 privates were dead, and two sergeant majors, four sergeants, a trumpeter and 123 private soldiers were wounded. Out of the initial casualty list of 275 all ranks, the final butcher's bill amounted to 263 KDG soldiers, showing how few of those posted as 'missing' ever rejoined the ranks unscathed. And, sadly for any cavalryman, 269 horses had been killed. More than half the regiment which had been present at Waterloo had been lost, 129 all ranks killed and 134 wounded.[1,6,9,29,30,31,32,33,34,35,36]

Sergeant Major Page, writing to his brother and sister, told them: 'Both the married men quartered with me at Romford were killed, one of them had three horses under him, and lost his life on a fourth, which was a French horse.'[13] Brigadier General Sir Hussey Vivian, commanding a light cavalry brigade, wrote: 'The Life Guards, Blues, with the 1st Dragoon Guards, gallantly met and repulsed the charges of the Cuirassiers in the very heat of the Action, and the losses of these Regiments afford evident proofs how severely they must have been engaged.'[9]

Trumpeter Wheeler ended his poem with these two verses:

But Now the Painful task Comes on I Am Sorry to Say
We Lost Many Noble officers Although we Gained the Day
Beside Some thousands of Our Men Lay bleeding On the Plains
And On the Minds of Britons their Deaths Will Long Remain.

But Now the battle Is over the Victory we have won
Fill up A Bumper And Drink A health unto Duke Wellington
Likewise the Earl of Uxbridge Lord Somerset Also
That led us On Like heroes On the Plains of Waterloo.[14]

FIVE

Aftermath and Pursuit

19 JUNE TO 7 JULY 1815

The late evening of 18 June had been fine and clear after the period of heavy rain, and this to some extent helped to relieve the sufferings of the wounded who covered the field of battle. Of the survivors of the Household Brigade bivouacked on the slope leading up to the French position, few felt any squeamishness at the terrible sights and sounds around them. They had endured a day surrounded by horror and carnage, and they were too tired to worry and too glad to be alive to be particular. Many may have felt like Mercer: 'I endeavoured to sleep. The cramped situation in which I lay, and the feverish excitement of my mind, forbade, however, my obtaining that sound and refreshing sleep so much needed – I only dozed. From one of these dozes I awoke about midnight, chilled and cramped to death from the awkward doubled-up position imposed upon me. So up I got to look around and contemplate a battle field by the pale moonlight. The night was serene and pretty clear; a few light clouds occasionally passing across the moon's disc, and throwing objects into transient obscurity, added considerably to the solemnity of the scene. Oh, it was a thrilling sensation thus to stand in the silent hour of the night and contemplate that field – all day long the theatre of noise and strife, now so calm and still – the actors prostrate on the bloody soil, their pale wan faces upturned to the moon's cold beams, which caps and breastplates, and a thousand other things, reflected back in brilliant pencils of light from as many different points. Here and there some poor wretch, sitting up amidst the countless dead, busied himself on efforts to staunch the flowing stream with which his life was fast ebbing away. Many whom I saw so employed that night were, when morning dawned, lying stiff and tranquil as those who had departed

74

earlier. From time to time a figure would half raise itself from the ground, and then, with a despairing groan, fall back again. Others, slowly and painfully rising, stronger, or having less deadly hurt, would stagger away with uncertain steps across the field in search of succour. Many of these I followed with my gaze until lost in the obscurity of distance; but many, alas! after staggering a few paces would sink again on the ground, probably to rise no more. It was heart rending – and yet I gazed! Horses, too, there were to claim our pity – mild, patient, enduring some lay on the ground with their entrails hanging out, and yet they lived. These would occasionally attempt to rise, but, like their human bedfellows, quickly falling back again, would lift their poor heads, and turning a wistful gaze at their side, lie quietly down, to repeat the same until strength no longer remained, and then, their eyes gently closing, one short convulsive struggle closed their sufferings. One poor animal excited painful interest – he had lost, I believe, both his hind legs; and there he sat the long night through on his tail, looking about, as if in expectation of coming aid, sending forth, from time to time, long and protracted melancholy neighing. Although I knew that killing him at once would be mercy, I could not muster courage even to give the order. Blood enough I had seen shed during the last thirty six hours, and sickened at the thought of shedding more. There, then, he still sat when we left the ground, neighing after us as if reproaching our desertion of him in the hour of need.'⁵

On this field of battle there lay some 40,000 men and 10,000 horses. Among the dead lay the dying and wounded. But for those who were still alive, it was not merely a matter of enduring the long chill hours of the night; with darkness came the looters, who did not hesitate to kill in their search for booty. Any of the wounded who resisted were at once stabbed or shot. Most of these nocturnal prowlers were British, Belgian or Prussian soldiers, who considered that stripping the fallen of their valuables was their just right. One wounded British officer recovered consciousness during the night and found that he could neither open his eyes nor move his legs – as if heavy weights were holding him down. His eyes were closed by dried blood and as he cleared them, he looked into the grinning face of a dead French soldier who was sprawled across him. A dead horse lay across his legs. A Prussian soldier paused to rob a nearby wounded officer, who resisted him and was promptly stabbed to death. Then the Prussian moved across and searched the dead Frenchman lying on the wounded officer's chest. Suddenly, the Prussian paused and listened, and then lay down feigning death. Two British looters approached and the officer called to them, and they came across and dragged the dead horse from off his feet and pulled aside the Frenchman. The officer begged them to stay with him but they could not as they had to return to their regiment, so he pointed out the Prussian playing dead, whom they killed at once, and then added his loot to their own. They gave the officer some brandy and a musket and left him.[26]

At daybreak Mercer records: 'The cool air of the morning lasted not long; the rising sun soon burst in all his glory over our bloody bivouac. The scene was now far from solitary; for numerous groups of peasants were moving about busily employed stripping the dead and perhaps finishing those not quite so. Some of these men I met fairly staggering under the enormous load of clothes, etc., they had collected. Some had firearms, swords, etc., and many had large bunches of crosses and decorations; all seemed in high glee, and professed unbounded hatred of the French. I stumbled on a whole regiment of British infantry fast asleep, in columns of division, wrapped in their blankets with their knapsacks for pillows. Not a man was awake. There they lay in regular ranks, with the officers and sergeants in their places, just as they would stand when awake.

'I was retracing my steps when my attention was called to a group of wounded Frenchmen by the calm dignified and soldier-like oration by one of them to the rest. The import was to exhort them to bear their sufferings with fortitude, but, above all, to remember that they were surrounded by Englishmen. The speaker was sitting on the ground, with his lance stuck upright beside him – an old veteran, with a thick bushy grizzly beard, countenance like a lion – a lancer of the Old Guard, and had no doubt fought in many a field. One hand was flourished in the air as he spoke, the other severed at the wrist, lay on the earth beside him; one ball (case-shot probably) had entered his body, another had broken his leg. His suffering, after a night of exposure so mangled, must have been great; yet he betrayed it not. I could not but feel the highest veneration for this brave man, and told him so, at the same time offering him the only consolation in my power – a drink of cold water, and assurances that the waggons would soon be sent round to collect the wounded. He thanked me with a grace peculiar to Frenchmen, and eagerly enquired the fate of their army. On this head I could tell him nothing consolatory, so merely answered that it had retired last night, and turned the conversation to the events of yesterday. This truly brave man spoke in most flattering terms of our troops. After a very interesting conversation, I begged his lance as a keepsake, observing that it could never be of further use to him. The old man's eyes kindled as I spoke and he emphatically assured me that it would delight him to see it in the hands of a brave soldier, instead of being torn from him, as he had feared, by those vile peasants. So I took my leave with the lance in my hand.'[5]

The battlefield presented such terrible sights that the Duke of Wellington rode back to Brussels. Sergeant Major Cotton records how 'solicitude for the wounded prompted him to request the assistance of the town authorities in collecting and removing the wounded from the field, as well as to restore confidence among the population, and alloy the extreme excitement which prevailed throughout Belgium. Right nobly did the inhabitants of Brussels respond to his appeal. The clergy, as might have been expected, were foremost in their exertions to relieve the dreadful agonies of so many gallant and innocent sufferers: the highest in rank rivalled the hardier classes in performing the most trying offices for the mangled heroes that filled the hospitals, and encumbered even many private dwellings. Ladies, of the honoured names of Merode and Robiano, set an illustrious example by their presence on the field the morning after the battle, the scene of carnage, so revolting to their delicate and tender nature, stimulating, instead of preventing, their humane exertions. Many other ladies, like ministering angels, shared in this work of mercy to the wounded, of whatever nation they might be, or in whatever cause they had fallen.'[15]

In Brussels Captain Naylor had found a place at the 'Hotel Grand Mirror'. The morning after the battle he was put in command of all the wounded of the King's Dragoon Guards in the depot of the wounded in Brussels, and he remained in charge until he had recovered from his own wound and left to rejoin the regiment on 2 July. Each day he visited Captain Turner who was lodged at the Hôtel de la Couronne d'Espagne. On the 20th Captain John Sweeney KDG and Lieutenant William Irvine KDG arrived in Brussels; both had been captured after the first charge at Waterloo, and both had managed to escape when the French retreated. Sweeney had been wounded and was lodged along with Turner at the Hôtel de la Couronne d'Espagne. Naylor remained in command of the depot until 2 July, when he handed over to Lieutenant John Gordon of the 18th Hussars. He attended the parade in the Park on Sunday 2 July and left Brussels at one o'clock in order to set out to rejoin the regiment.[3]

Meanwhile, that morning of 19 June, the curious and the sightseers began to arrive on the battlefield. Mercer tells how 'a carriage drove on the field from Brussels, the inmates of which alighting, proceeded to examine the field. It was amusing to see the horror with which they eyed our frightful figures; they all, however, pulled off their hats and made us long bows. One, a smartly dressed middle-aged man, in a high cocked hat, entered into conversation with one on the events of yesterday. He approached holding a delicately white perfumed handkerchief to his nose; stepping carefully to avoid the bodies (at which he cast fearful glances en passant), to avoid polluting the glossy silken hose that clothed his nether limbs. With a world of bows my man took leave, and proceeded picking his steps, with the same care, as he followed the route of his companions.'[5]

Officers and men strolled about asking each other not who was dead, but who was still alive. The local Belgian parish priests made their churches into hospitals, and one local brewer drove his dray loaded with beer to the battlefield. The wounded soon drank his entire supply. In spite of all that was done it was days before all the wounded were attended to, and in spite of Wellington's order that all wounded were to be succoured irrespective of nationality, individual regiments tended to care for their own and other British soldiers first.[26,27]

John Hibbert wrote home: 'You may conceive what a slaughter it was, when we lost five entire troops out of eight, so that now we only muster three. Poor Barnard [sic, brother of Cornet Bernard KDG] of the Scotch Greys, formerly of our regiment, is killed; we all regret him more than any officer of our own regiment. Their regiment also suffered as much as ours; they lost fifteen officers – eight killed, the rest wounded and missing. The French lost about eighty thousand men, killed and prisoners, we lost about forty thousand including foreign troops.'[2]

In a later letter he wrote: 'This time last year in Ireland, before the reductions, we mustered in the field eleven hundred men – a thousand effective. Now the whole regiment cannot muster three hundred including the depot, and about two hundred and fifty horses, and all our best and worthiest officers killed. It is very singular but really those officers who were the most respected and liked in the regiment, are all killed; in fact the regiment will never be what it was. Colonel Fuller and the Adjutant, Captain Battersby, Majors Graham and Bringhurst and Lieutenant Brook were all thrown into one grave and buried by the Thirty Second regiment. Young Barnard's [sic] body could not be found, but we know pretty well what became of him; he was taken prisoner after having been wounded, and not being able to keep up with the French, they killed him on the road. They served a great many English officers in the same way; their retreat was extremely rapid.

'The Scotch Greys lost about half their regiment. The most melancholy thing is that no sooner were our poor men wounded than the Belgic troops, who were without exception the greatest set of cowards and rascals in the world, stript them of everything but their shirts and left them in this miserable way all night. Our officers were only known by the name on their shirts; I daresay many died of cold in the night. Our brigade was so totally cut up that a party could not be mustered that night to go over the ground and consequently the wounded men and officers were left to shift for themselves. Such a scene of misery was never seen before; the action took place about eighteen miles from Brussels, and the road was strewed with dead men the whole way, who had been trying to crawl to the town from the field and had died on the road, some through cold, others through hunger and thirst. For the space of six miles (beginning from the field of battle and going over the road that the French had retreated) the way was literally so strewed with bodies of horses and men that no carriage or horse could pass unless they went considerably to the right or left. I fancied it was in the time of the Romans, for all the French were clad in complete armour of steel, and were lying in piles one on the other; this was two days after the battle, for the French were not pursued by the English after the battle, but by the Prussians who came up just as the battle was finished. The Prussians kept up a continual fire on the retreating French and consequently killed as many English prisoners as Frenchmen.

'The truth is this (whatever they may say in the newspaper), that if it had not been for the timely arrival of the Prussians, not an Englishman would have escaped, for although the French might have retreated that night, they would have renewed the contest next morning and no doubt their numbers would have prevailed, for our army was scattered in all directions even after having gained victory. The Prussians would give no quarter, but killed every wounded man on the road, neither would they receive any.'[2]

Wellington's despatch written to the Secretary of State on the day after the battle, and published in the *London Gazette* on 22 June, paid tribute to the part played by the King's Dragoon Guards. He wrote: 'The enemy repeatedly charged our infantry with his cavalry, but these attacks were uniformly unsuccessful and they afforded opportunities to our cavalry to charge, in one of which Lord E. Somerset's brigade, consisting of the Life Guards, Royal Horse Guards, and 1st Dragoon Guards, highly distinguished themselves, as did that of Major General Sir W. Ponsonby, having taken many prisoners and an eagle.'[37]

Marshal Blücher's Official Report also stated: 'The English

Army fought with a valour which it is impossible to surpass. The repeated charges of the Old Guard were baffled by the intrepidity of the Scottish regiments; and at every charge the French cavalry were overthrown by the English cavalry. But the superiority of the enemy in numbers was too great; Napoleon continually brought forward considerable masses, and with whatever firmness the English troops maintained themselves in their position, it was not possible but that such heroic exertions must have a limit.'[22]

John Hibbert had missed the actions on 17 and 18 June, and rejoined the regiment two days after the battle on the 20th. He was sensitive to the fact that he had missed the fighting and explained why in a letter to his mother. 'About a fortnight ago, te n days before the Regiment marched, I and a party of officers to pass away the time, erected a leaping bar in a field near Denderleur. We all brought our horses without saddles into the field for the purpose of trying which could leap best. I rode at the bar, which was about four feet high, and after clearing it, my mare made a sudden swerve to the left, and threw me off, in consequence of which I was laid up with a swelling in the groin owing to the strain, and I never left my room for the first three days. The pain was so great that I could not eat anything and in consequence I was reduced to a most miserable state, and to add to my comfort, I was attacked by boils breaking out all over my body. In fact I was unable to do duty – and every officer in the regiment will say the same – so that I am not in the least ashamed of not having been in the engagement. I was just getting better when the regiment marched, and the night before, poor Barnard –and another officer came to see me, and they agreed to dine with me next day – so little idea they had of marching. An orderly dragoon came with the despatch at three the next morning, and the whole regiment were off by five; when I awoke, my man Oliver told me the regiment was gone, and that no order had been left for me.

'I remained at Denderleur that day, and the next, which was the 17th. I set off in a cabriolet to a small town called Nenof [Ninove] I there enquired of the Commissary General what I was to do, and how I could proceed. He told me my best way would be to go to Brussels, so accordingly I set off on the 19th in a cabriolet, and arrived there about six in the evening. I there met with two of our officers who told me of the battle and the fate of the regiment. You may conceive my astonishment when I learned that only one troop survived and almost all the officers killed. I set out with them the next day and joined the remainder of the regiment a few miles from Genappe; I might have remained at Brussels and returned myself sick, but I thought I should be well in a few days and therefore I was determined to join before they went further. I was plagued with boils all the march, and I could do nothing to them as we bivouacked all the way; latterly I was so ill that I was obliged to go in the hospital waggon with the sick men, and I never got completely rid of them until about a week after my arrival here (Paris). Many officers and men were attacked with the same complaint, owing to the heat of the climate. I would rather have been in twenty battles than again undergo the misery that I endured.

'I joined on the 20th and we expected to be engaged everyday until we got here; such a retreat was never known before. I would give a great deal had I seen and been in the engagement of the 18th, but accidents will happen to all people at different times. My consolation is that every officer and man knew that I was unable to do any duty whatever at the time the regiment marched, for I suppose you are aware of what some ill-natured people might say.'[2]

The Household Cavalry Brigade, having bivouacked on the battlefield after the battle, did not move far on the following day, 19 June. Wellington marched the army from the battlefield to Nivelles which gave Lieutenant Hibbert and others time to rejoin near Genappe. But then the pursuit speeded up. On the 20th Binch was reached, Malplaquet on the 21st and Cateau Cambresis on the 22nd; on the 23rd the troops were allowed to rest. By 25 June Wellington established his headquarters at Jattcourt, and the army was beyond Vermant on the 26th. On 28 June Blücher's forces were in front of St Denis and Vincennes and on this day Napoleon left Paris. On 29 June John Hibbert wrote to his mother from within fifteen miles of Paris. 'I received your letters yesterday and blame myself greatly for not writing sooner, but there certainly is an excuse for we have been undergoing the greatest hardships since I wrote last. We march for twenty to thirty miles everyday, up always at three o'clock and sleep all night in the fields, for we lost all our tents and most part of our baggage. I have done this now for sometime and feel no inconvenience from it.'[2]

Mercer had some comments to make on Prussian looting. 'We rather unexpectedly entered a pretty village – that is, it had been once so; now devastation had visited it, and the forelorn deserted street was everywhere encumbered as usual with broken glass and fragments of furniture etc., every window in the place was destroyed. In front of the church was a small open space, whence a handsome lodge and grille gave a view of a long avenue terminated by a chateau. In this place about twenty or thirty hussar horses were standing linked together under charge of one hussar. I believe these people were Prussians, but I can't say. From this man we learned that his companions were at the chateau, and thither we went curious to ascertain what they did there. We were certainly not quite so much shocked at the scenes of ruin and havoc which presented itself as we went down the avenue, as we should have been a week ago; they are becoming familiar now. The fragments of sofas, chairs, tables, etc, lying about the grass, bespoke a richly furnished house, and the nearer we drew to the house the thicker became these signs of vengeance. Large pieces of painted paper torn from the walls, remnants of superb silk window-curtains, with their deep rich fringe, hung among the bushes; broken mirrors and costly lustres covered the ground in such a manner as to render it difficult to avoid hurting our horses' feet; slabs of the rarest marble, torn from the chimney-pieces, lay shattered to atoms; even the beds had been ripped open, and the contents given to the winds, and conveyed by them to all parts of the park, covering in some places the ground like newly fallen snow. The trees of the avenue were cut and hacked, and large patches of bark torn off – many were blackened and scorched by fires made at the foot of them, with the mahogany furniture for fuel; the shrubs cut down or torn up by the roots; the very turf itself turned up or trampled into mud by the feet of men and horses. I dismounted at the grand entrance. Shouts and laughter resounded through the building. The hussars were busy completing the work of destruction; and as we passed the magnificent stairs leading up the hall, we narrowly escaped being crushed under a large mirror which these gentlemen at that very moment launched over the banisters above with loud cheers. The rooms had been most luxuriously and richly furnished; now they were empty, the papering hanging in rags from the walls, and even the cornices destroyed more or less. Every kind of abuse of France and the French was written on the walls. In one room was the remnants of a grand piano. The next room seemed to have been chosen as the place of execution of all the porcelain in the house, which had there been collected for a grand smash. The handsomest Sèvres and Dresden vases, tea and dinner services, formed fragments all over the floor, and a large porcelain stove had shared the same fate. Another room had been lined with mirrors from the ceiling to the floor; it appeared these had been made targets of, for many were the marks of pistol-balls on the walls they had covered. On enquiring of one hussar why they had so particularly wrecked their vengeance on this house, he said it belonged to Jerome Buonaparte, whom every German detested. Having seen enough here, we looked into another chateau somewhat smaller, but which had also been something very fine; it was precisely in the same state. Disgusted we returned to our garden.'[5]

It was not only the Prussians who offended Mercer's sense of tolerance. 'A party of Dutch broke into the church, and after amusing themselves for a time with dressing themselves in the priest's garments, etc., and turning into ridicule the Roman Catholic ceremonies, finished by breaking to pieces the altar and destroying everything they found in the church or vestry. Our allies are by no means an amiable set, nor very cordial with us. If an English corps occupy a chateau and its grounds, still they leave free ingress and egress to any others so long as they do not interfere with them. On the contrary, a single Dutch Nassau or

Belge will sometimes (if a commanding officer) occupy a whole place himself: sentinels are placed at every gate and the place strictly tabooed. They are a brutal set. The Dutch appear the best. They are all uncommonly insolent to us.'5

Captain Naylor, on his way from Brussels to rejoin the regiment, had the same experience. 'I then got into a Prussian baggage waggon and advanced slowly to Louvres where we were so fortunate as to procure a fresh cart and horses. All the villages from Noyon were entirely deserted, having been pillaged by the Prussians, who had marched on that route. Windows broken, doors forced open, furniture destroyed – nothing but misery.'3

John Hibbert took a more sympathetic view of Prussian excesses. 'The Prussians got beat the other day,' he wrote to his father. 'The French made an attack on them very unexpectedly, and after killing many, retreated over the bridge and blew it up, so that the Prussians had not an opportunity of revenging themselves. The hatred that exists between the two nations is astonishing; the French shudder at the very name of the Prussian, who plunder and burn wherever they go, and spare nothing. This retaliation is perfectly just, for the French committed much more atrocious deeds when they were in Prussia. You may imagine what comfortable work it was following their troops who were a day's march before us; nothing but the bare walls of houses, not a soul in the villages, and nothing but water to be had – not a bit of bread, if you were to give your life for it. I was the only one who had a gun and therefore managed very well; at least I thought myself well off if I killed a tough old pigeon and boiled him into soup. One day we found, concealed in a barn, fourteen barrels of excellent claret; you may conceive how we regaled ourselves.'2

As the King's Dragoon Guards advanced through northern France they hoped to get news of some of the officers and men who had been posted as 'missing', for it was known that many had been made prisoners, especially those who had reached the French Great Battery in the first charge on 18 June. John Hibbert tells what happened. 'None of our officers that were returned missing have as yet made an appearance; therefore there is no doubt that they were killed. What prisoners of our regiment were taken, we certainly believe to have been murdered in cool blood by the French on their retreat. A sergeant major of ours was taken prisoner at Waterloo and the other day he was discovered lying dead with his head split open, and about seven men of our regiment with him, in a small wood eight miles from this place. He was the fattest man in the regiment, and we suppose he must have knocked up, for they used them shamefully, driving them on with their bayonets and giving them nothing to eat or drink the whole day. Added to this they stripped them of everything they had except their overalls and shirts, and some had nothing but a blanket to cover them. No wonder our poor fellow knocked up with this usage; we wonder how he got as far as he did, but he knew there was but one alternative and that when he gave in, he was to die. Poor young Barnard perished in the same manner we suppose, for his body was not found in the field, and what adds to this distressing circumstance is that his mother died the other day in consequence of the news.'[2]

The advance, made at speed in the height of summer, had been gruelling. John Hibbert told his sister how 'from the time we set out from Denderleur to the time when we got near Valencinnes [sic], we halted two days; the first day I dedicated entirely to sleep, the second I was bad and made myself look as decent as possible, but I was a sorry figure after all my pains. You may conceive a person with a shirt of a week's wearing on, a dirty handkerchief, for I cannot call it black, overalls torn in eleven places, a jacket any colour but red, and to crown it all a beard that hung down to the breast, and a helmet without a tail. This was the costume of most of our officers.

'These two days we had a barn to lie in – a great luxury. It was the first we had had from the time we set out, for so great was the army in persuit of the French that it was impossible to find quarters for them. The cavalry fared worse than the infantry for their baggage and tents could not keep up with them, therefore we were always obliged to bivouac excepting the instance which I mentioned. The weather was very fine, with the exception of three nights when it did rain cats and dogs. We had not then got into the proper method of building our houses, so that for three successive nights I got wet through and through, but never found any inconvenience from it; I mean in the way of catching cold. All this time we had nothing to eat but biscuit, and sometimes a bit of miserable cow that had been driven by dint of whip twenty six miles a day; the worst part of the business was that we could not get good water.

'We always marched about three in the morning or thereabouts and got to our bivouac about five, sometimes sooner. If there was time, I used to get a carbine and cut up some bullets to make shot, and so set out a-shooting pigeons, for there were vast quantities about the fields. While I was shooting, another officer was building the house and boiling potatoes etc., if we could get them. This was all very good fun while the weather was fair, but when it rained I cannot describe the misery we endured.

'I will give you an idea of one night. It had been raining the whole of the day but cleared up a little when we came to our bivouac, so we began a house upon the square plan, (instead of this form △ which we afterwards found to be the proper one) and finished it off as well as we could. The ground was as wet as it could be, and the hedge which formed the back part of the house was no less so. Brander [Lieutenant Thomas Brander KDG] and I were together that night and very luckily we found a hen's nest with seventeen eggs in it in a cornfield. It was a great Godsend. We of course told nobody of it, for there was no harm in being selfish at this time – "Every man for himself" was the word – so when we had made ourselves a little comfortable by drying some green corn by a large fire and then spreading it in the house to lie upon, our saddles for pillows, and our large cloak for covering – when we had done all this, we boiled the eggs and congratulated ourselves on the prospect of a good dinner. Fortunately I had a little brandy in a bottle which I always carried about with me; this was a great addition to our intended meal, for we never came to eating of the business as you will soon find.

'When the eggs were boiled, the punch made, and the first egg broke, what should surprise us but a sudden discharge of musketry. We were exceedingly astonished, as we supposed the French were at least six leagues from us, however, little time was given to think, for the bugle immediately sounded the turn out, the dinner was all put aside and never thought of, we flew to saddle our horses (for we had no servants, they being with the baggage). We soon finished although it was as dark as pitch and nothing but the light of fires to see by; the regiment was formed in a minute and we marched out of the field, every minute expecting to be attacked. Suddenly the bugle sounded the halt, and a dragoon came up to the Commandant and informed him that the firing was nothing more than some Belgic troops discharging their pieces after the rain, so of course we were ordered back to our bivouac. We cursed the Belgians and the muskets and wished them all to the devil, and in this temper returned, and expected to find the dinner as we had left it in our house. In vain did we look for our eggs and punch – not the slightest remains of it could we see, and so we stood in no very good temper musing on our forlorn condition. Just at this moment there came down from the heavens the most infernal shower of rain I ever witnessed; in five minutes we were wet through our cloaks. The house was no protection but rather increased our misery, for it was composed of branches; the wet dripped from them all night, long after the rain had ceased. I had still some brandy and biscuits left, and we comforted ourselves as well as we could. Thus ended our agreeably spent night. I laugh at it now it's all over, but I rather think if anybody had laughed at me then, he would not have got off with whole bones!'[2]

On 29 June John Hibbert wrote to his mother: 'We shall enter Paris tomorrow, but not without a little fighting, as the Prussians attempted it and were repulsed, so says a report. I am perfectly well and I hope I shall see you soon. I am now writing under a little house made of the boughs of trees; the weather is extremely hot and therefore this sort of life is not unpleasant. The worst part of the business is that there is no getting anything to eat, the Prussians having plundered all the villages before us. I shot a hare yesterday by great luck, which will serve me for breakfast and dinner for sometime.'[2]

In fact Paris was not entered for another week. The broken ground around Versailles enabled the French to ambush the

Prussians on 1 July, but the following day a strong Prussian attack got them as far as Issy. On the 3rd the French advanced from Paris to try to retake Issy, but were repulsed. It was then that a French flag of truce appeared with the news that Paris was ready to surrender. Wellington and Blücher met the French delegates at St Cloud and a convention was signed on the 4th ending the war, and the Allied army entered Paris on 7 July.

Meanwhile, on 1 July Mercer, whose battery was back with the Household Cavalry Brigade, noted that 'Another reinforcement has joined us. That beautiful but unfortunate regiment, the Cumberland Hussars, has been broken up for its retrograde movement on the 18th, and distributed among the different corps. Being all gentlemen from Hanover, it is easy to imagine they are rather irate at this degradation.

'Lord Edward [Somerset] ordered a sale today of the effects of the slain. This occasioned a little stir in the village, and passed away an hour or two. I have purchased a good large cloak, erst the property of poor Colonel Fuller of the 1st Dragoon Guards. Things sold well in general.'[5]

On 8 July the King of France, Louis XVIII entered Paris. Sergeant Stubbings wrote to his parents the following day: 'Bonepart is completely defeted and Lewis the 18th entered Paires yesterday and Whee expect all the fitting is over which I hope it is for it is Dredfule to relate the scens I saw on the 18th.'[18]

SIX

The Occupation of Paris

7 JULY 1815 TO 7 MAY 1816

The King's Dragoon Guards entered Paris with the British army on 7 July and went into quarters at Nanterre.[1] John Hibbert wrote: 'We are comfortably situated within five miles of Paris and expect to remain here until affairs are settled.'[2]

In the meantime James Naylor, having recovered from his wounds, was on his way back to rejoin the regiment. He left Brussels at 1 p.m. on Sunday 2 July and reached Braine le Comte by four and Mons by seven o'clock, where he dined with someone called Fairholme and slept the night in billets. The name Fairholme does not appear in the Army List and he may have been a civilian friend, many of whom did cross to Belgium and France. The next morning, having breakfasted, Naylor travelled with his friend by chaise to Bavay, got some wine, bread and cheese at a cottage, and then only with difficulty managed to procure a cart to take him to Cateau.

They arrived there by 9 p.m., had a meal at an inn, and spent the night again in billets. On 4 July Fairholme and Naylor breakfasted together; then with Fairholme travelling in a cart and Naylor riding, they journeyed to Cambrai. The countryside was open, and covered in corn, with villages here and there, but no woods or enclosures. At Cambrai, 'a large town', they ate a hurried dinner and then went on by diligence to St Quentin for supper and a bed. They left by coach at 5 a.m., having been joined by an officer of the Chasseurs Britanniques and having been given passports to proceed by the Prussian Commandant of St Quentin. They stopped for breakfast for two hours at Hane, and before moving off for Noyon their driver forced them to make a new bargain to take them on to Compiègne. They arrived at 5 p.m. and visited the hunting chateau of the French Royal Family and wandered through its grounds.

On Thursday 6 July they set out at 4 a.m. in a diligence for Senlis, which they reached in time for breakfast. Travelling now began to get more difficult. They managed to hire some post horses and eventually an old cart, but that broke down soon after they left, so they transferred to a Prussian baggage wagon and proceeded slowly to Louvres, where they found a cart and fresh horses. By now Naylor and Fairholme, who was travelling with a servant, had been joined by two French officers, and they also got their first news of the whereabouts of the Household Cavalry Brigade, which was bivouacked at Roissy. They made their way there in time to dine with the 2nd Life Guards, and the following day, 7 July, Naylor rejoined the regiment in time to march from Roissy at 4 a.m.. They crossed a pontoon bridge over the River Seine and reached Nanterre where Naylor slept in his billet.

Within a few days the King's Dragoon Guards marched from Nanterre to new billets at Rouelle. John Hibbert, who spells Rouelle variously as 'Rouel', 'Reuil', 'Roule', wrote on 15 July to his sister: 'Dear Tiddle, we are still in our former quarters within five miles of Paris, and I do not think there is any great chance of our moving at present. The weather is extremely hot and therefore we travel in cabriolets when we go to Paris, Versailles, St Cloud etc., for I have made it a point to see all these places, and likewise everything worth seeing in them. We are now in the height of luxury – nothing to do but eat, drink and sleep, pleasures which we have long been strangers to.'[2]

The events of the past month still loomed fresh. Hibbert comments: 'I am sorry that the Greys and Inniskillings were not mentioned in the papers for they behaved very well. This was the only action in which our regiment was engaged; there was a slight skirmish on the 17th in which the Highland brigade of infantry suffered much. This attack was chiefly sustained by the foreign troops – I call it a skirmish when put in comparison with the battle of the 18th, for such a one was never fought before, or ever will be again, I hope. There was no fighting after the 18th excepting that the Prussians fired a few shots at Paris. The report is at present that Bony has concentrated his army in the south, and has got at least a hundred thousand men. We do not know what to believe; I do not think the business is over yet.'[2]

On 26 July Hibbert wrote to his father: 'I am still in the same place (Rouelle). But expect now to march every day to the Loire to subdue the remains of the Bony's army, who swear they won't give up. We have heard of Bony's capture long ago; we have not heard of it officially but it is generally supposed to be true. There certainly will be another battle, at least so it is asserted, some say we shall have nothing to do with it, but will leave it all to the Allies, but this report has proved false, for some English regiments marched today, both cavalry and infantry.'[2]

On 24 July the Duke of Wellington reviewed the Allied army in Paris, together with the Czar Alexander, the Emperor of Austria, the King of Prussia and Louis XVIII, newly restored King of France. At this review none of the heavy cavalry regiments carried their standards. The two heavy cavalry brigades had been ordered, before leaving England, to leave them at home. John Hibbert related how 'we mustered forty thousand and made a remarkably fine review. We were on the right of the line and therefore got home soon, but those on the left did not pass the Emperors until eight in the evening; it was a tedious business for them, for they were on the ground at six in the morning.'[2]

Mercer, being horse artillery attached to the Household Cavalry Brigade, also 'marched early, as the line was to be formed by nine o'clock. We had a long and tedious wait; and as the day was very hot, it was no small treat to discover that an apothecary hard by had some excellent raspberry vinegar, which, I think, we exhausted. At length the approach of the sovereigns was announced, and they came preceded and followed by a most numerous and brilliant cortège, in which figured, perhaps, some of almost every arm of every army in Europe. It was a splendid and most interesting sight. First came the Emperor Alexander and the King of Prussia, in their respective green and blue uniforms, riding together – the former, as usual, all smiles; the latter taciturn and melancholy. A little in their rear followed the Austrian Emperor, in a white uniform, turned up with red, but quite plain – a thin, dried-up, thread-paper of a man, not of the most distinguished bearing; his lean brown visage, however, bore an expression of kindness and bonhommie, which folk say his true character in no way belies. They passed along, scanning our people with evident interest and curiosity; and in passing me (as they did to every Commanding Officer) pulled off their hats and saluted me with most gracious smiles. I wonder if they do the same to their own.

'Our infantry – indeed, our whole army – appeared at the review in the same clothes in which they had marched, slept, and fought for months. The colour had faded to a dusky brick-dust hue; their coats, originally not very smartly made, had acquired by constant wearing that loose easy set so characteristic of old clothes, comfortable to the wearer, but not calculated to add grace to his appearance. Pour surcroit de laideur, their cap is perhaps the meanest, ugliest thing ever invented. From all these causes it arose that our infantry appeared to the utmost disadvantage – dirty, shabby, mean and very small. Some such impression was, I fear, made on the sovereigns for a report has reached us this morning, that they remarked to the Duke what very small men the English were. "Ay", replied our noble chief, "they are small; but your Majesties will find none who fight so well."'

'At length they finished, and, taking their stand in the Place Louis Quinze, we marched past in columns of division. The crowd assembled to witness this exceeding anything I had ever seen before. Not only were the people packed as thick as they could stand in the area itself, but the buildings of the Garde Meuble, the ramparts of the Tuileries, even the roof of the Hotel Bourbon over the river, were all crowded – windows, roofs, and every cornice that could hold human beings. After passing, we took our route along the Rue Royale Boulevard and Rue Poissoniere, starting off at a good trot, and got home about six o'clock.'[5]

Mercer also described the billets of the various British troops. 'The greater part of our cavalry is, I believe, on the left bank of the Seine. The Life Guards, Blues etc. are at Nanterre, Rueil etc., Hussars at Suresnes, Puteaux etc. The 12th, and another light dragoon regiment, at Courbevoie in the fine barracks.'[5]

John Hibbert commented: 'It is ridiculous to hear the praise

An officer of the 1st King's Dragoon Guards.
A French artist's impression painted during the occupation
by J. Duplessi Bertaux c.1816, and published in Paris.

that the English newspapers give the foreign troops. They say that the Duke of Brunswick was killed gallantly charging at the head of his troops. So far from it, that his troops (that is his cavalry) never charged at all; as soon as they came within twenty years of the French they turned tail and fled, and left their General to the mercy of these rascals, who after defending himself for some time, got killed by a Lancer. In vain he waved his sword in the air, and cheered his men; he was too brave to follow their example, and so literally charged into their lines by himself.

'I have seen everything in Paris worth seeing and have now devoted my time principally to shooting. The game is in great quantities here; I killed six brace and a half of partridges in less than two hours the other day . . . I am sorry to say that the Louvre is no longer worth a person going to see: the Allies have dismantled it terribly. The Venus de Medicis and the Apollo, with many of the principal statues, are on their return to their native countries; there are very few pictures left, however I saw it in its prime four days after the capitulation. They have taken the horses from the Triumphal Car and sent them back to Venice. You have heard perhaps of the celebrated Triumphal Arch that Bony built at the Tuilleries, upon the top of which was a splendid car and four horses of bronze originally as large as life annexed to it? These he brought from Venice where they were very much celebrated for their beauty and antiquity. But he entirely spoiled them by gilding them over to match the car which was built in Paris. This looks very foolish without the horses.

'There is also a beautiful pillar in the Place Vendome which you might have heard of, built entirely of brass cannon taken by the French at the Battle of Austerlitz; it is the most beautiful thing I ever saw. The Emperor of Austria swears that he will never leave France until that pillar of his disgrace is taken down; therefore it is to be removed for the cannon were all cast into a beautiful representation of the battle. It is again to be cast into cannon and the Emperor will conduct them once again into Austria. It is a very grating thing to the French to see these things done; and the English soldiers keeping guard at the Tuilleries and not allowing a Frenchman even to go near the Louvre – still more hard.

'We all expect a devil of a kick-up soon, but if such a thing should happen, Paris will be burnt to a certainty; everybody says that this will be the end of that city, and very shortly. There have been very great disturbances lately. Every evening there is a crowd under poor (King) Louis' window at the Tuilleries, and "Vive l'Empereur" sung out under his very nose. If the poor man comes out to expostulate, which he does now and then, his eye is immediately bunged up with a rotten egg, and he departs in peace. I believe if the Allies were to leave Paris, he would be murdered immediately, and if Bony was to make his appearance there is not a man who would not side with him, and really no wonder.'[2]

Later in the autumn Hibbert wrote to his father: 'Paris is very quiet at present. Four regiments sleep under arms every night in case of disturbance, and are not more than three hundred yards from the Tuilleries where they are encamped, so that Louis sleeps in peace – a thing he would not do if the Allies were away, left to the mercy of his own subjects.'[2]

Mercer did not take such a gloomy view of Paris; he was fascinated by the sights, but more particularly by the people. 'Our champagne was excellent and very cheap. In England we should pay from ten shillings to fifteen shillings per bottle. This cost me precisely five francs, or 4/2d. a bottle – some little difference. Rode to Paris. When I arrived, there were several people in the stable, who gathered around me and (my horse) Cossack, asking with apparent curiosity if he was in the battle. I told them Yes, and all about his eight wounds – the scars of which were visible enough. This seemed to excite great interest; and I walked off, leaving them assembled round the fellow's stall, having first, however, warned them of his heels. The Palais Royal, Rue Vivienne, and Boulevard were the scenes of my promenade. The Rue Vivienne is a kind of Bond Street. Like Bond Street, it is narrow. In London, this narrow badly-paved avenue, with its gutter down the centre, would only rank as a lane. Here is to be seen all the beauty and fashion of Paris. If some of the fashionable shops under the arcades of the Palais Royal are more splendid, the articles in these are more substantially rich and good. The Boulevards (for there are many) form a sort of circular road round what once was Paris, separating it from the Faubourgs, and these Boulevards form a street about as broad as Oxford Street, perhaps broader. This is the most amusing part of Paris. The road is incessantly thronged with carts, fiacres, cabriolets, private equipages and horse-men; every now and then a detachment of gens d'armes is seen urging them their way soberly through the crowd. But it is the footway one finds the greater source of amusement. Here one meets promenaders or passengers in every variety of European, and even some Asiatic, costumes. Some by their lounging gait, are employed only in killing time; others bustling from shop to shop are people whose money burns in their pockets, and their amusement consists in getting rid of it as quickly as possible for articles utterly useless to them. Again, a third, and by far the most numerous, are people whose pockets burn to have money in them.

'My great torment in the Boulevard is a little wretch of a girl, about ten or twelve years old, whose ostensible business is the sale of toothpicks, but in reality is begging. This little animal fixes herself on one with the tenacity of a leech – running by one's side, occasionally holding up the articles of her pretended trade, and unceasingly plying her song. And then when she becomes convinced of the inutility of perseverance, suddenly stopping and entering into an indifferent, perhaps merry, confab with some chum, and again starting after some other likely looking customer.'[5]

John Hibbert, on the other hand, was becoming more and more disillusioned with garrison life in France. He wrote to his sister: 'I am not certain of getting leave of absence on the plea of ill-health. I shall not be strong enough to travel for a fortnight or three weeks; I have been much worse than I have given you any reason to suppose, but now that I am getting better it does not matter. My rheumatism proceeded from bathing in the Seine when I was in a perspiration. It attacked me in the chest and I could hardly breathe. I worked this off by violent exercise, but it returned and attacked me in my hand, leg etc. In fact I have been confined six weeks and am greatly reduced, as you may easily imagine. Many of our officers have been ill; fevers are very common owing to the men eating quantities of grapes and drinking bad wine, for they get claret of inferior quality here for five pence a bottle. I shall be glad to return to my native air; the nasty French dishes do not agree with me. In fact I am heartily sick of France and everything appertaining thereunto.'[2]

In October he followed this up. 'You deservedly censure me for not dating my letters, but the fact is as you suppose – I very seldom recollect the day of the month, and as my quarters are at some distance from any others, I have not an opportunity of enquiring of any person except my man Oliver, who generally proves as stupid as his master in this respect. You also accuse me of six weeks silence, but I have a good excuse for this; I really was incapable of writing for five weeks – my hand was continuously bandaged up, as I mentioned in my last letter. Today has been the fourth day that I have ventured out of my room; I get stronger every day and I shall immediately apply for leave.'[2]

Hibbert must have applied and been disappointed, for on 2 December he wrote to his father: 'I have applied for leave and it has been refused; if anyone had bet me a thousand pounds to a shilling that I should not obtain it, I would not have believed him. An officer of the name of Hawley and myself went before the Board of Health last Tuesday but one, held at St. Denis, and from the nature of the certificates we got from the regimental surgeon specifying that it was necessary we should go to England, we had no doubt of getting leave. About four days afterwards our Colonel sent us two letters from the Adjutant General, in which we found that Lord Wellington had granted us each a month's leave, but where to? To St. Denis, there to remain under the every day inspection of the rascally staff surgeons until we had recovered our health, and then to join our regiment. Upon reading this, I wrote to the Adjutant General saying that as St. Denis was only four miles from Ruelle, and as our surgeon had recommended my native air as necessary to the re-establishment of my health, I begged he would erase my name from the sick list and allow me to join the regiment at Ruelle, as there could be no great difference in the air, where the places were only four miles apart.'[2]

Sergeant Stubbings was worried about his letters. 'Dear father I sent you a letter 2 Months since and I have received No anser which Makes Me unesy as I Sent My Watch when I Left England by Corporal Ropers Wife and it Gives Me Unesines about it and I hope you will inform Me Whether you received it or not as I hope you have before this time Give My Kind Love to them all and inform them that I ham well after Such Sharp fiting and Long Marching – When you wright which I hope will be on Receipt of this Direct for Me.'[18]

John Hibbert was also concerned about those things that one would expect to matter to young officers – chances of promotion, pay, and the state of the regiment. Just before Waterloo he had written to his mother: 'It was the most lucky thing in the world that I purchased the lieutenancy, for George Quicke, who refused the purchase, has had no less than nine lieutenants put over him, so that he is now in a worse situation than when he joined, for as we are upon the war establishment we have twenty-four lieutenants and he is at the bottom of all these, and consequently will get reduced when we return home to a certainty, for the promotion can never be so quick as to get him out of the break. I have not seen an army list lately, but I rather think I am thirteenth lieutenant, consequently not safe, but it is odd if there is not a single promotion in the regiment before we return, for one would get me completely out of the scrape.'[2]

After the battle, on the road to Paris, he wrote to his mother: 'I shall be pretty high among the lieutenants; I wish you would copy the promotions of our regiment out of the army list, in your next letter.' But in October he was telling his father: 'You mention in your letter that you think it an extraordinary thing that a man from the infantry should be put into the regiment as Captain in preference to Hawley who is senior lieutenant. It certainly has been the case hitherto that in case of vacancies occurring by officers being killed in action, the promotion goes in the regiment, but it seems that they have made an innovation upon this rule by not allowing more than three troops to go in the regiment. We had four vacancies, and we thought it very lucky that three went in the regiment. No instance has ever occurred where cavalry suffered so severely as on the 18th and I hope never will again.'[2]

On the subject of pay, there was a period on first arrival in Belgium when pay did not come through. By 11 June, however, Hibbert could report: 'Tell Father that we received all the pay due to us the other day, and therefore I shall be enabled to go on without drawing on England.' But by the end of July he was finding life in Paris rather more expensive: 'I drew the other day for £50, which draft an officer in our regiment was so good as to ask for me at the usual rate of exchange. I found my pay quite insufficient to defray my expenses here, for I had to get many new things of different descriptions, and we do not get pay regularly but sometimes are a month in arrears.'[2]

His letters show a true cavalryman's concern: 'I have been more lucky in my horses than any man in the regiment. I have always had four and never had one unfit to ride since I came into the country except in one instance. Other officers have had two sore backs out of three horses on the average. If once a horse gets his skin off his back on the march, it is all over with him; I have seen holes on horses' backs that you might put your fist in, in three days from the time that the skin was first rubbed off, notwithstanding this, they were obliged to carry the baggage, for officers had no money to purchase others. I owe my good luck to my servant Oliver who is an excellent groom. The black mare I had at Birtels had never failed in the least; I have never rode any other horse or charger, or ever will as long as I am in this country. I was offered eighty guineas for her the other day, but refused it, for when a person has a good horse, he ought never to part with it, and I never will with her. When she is done with, you can turn her out in the sawpit field, and there let her end her days.'[2]

On 25 October Hibbert wrote to his father: 'The general opinion is that we shall return home this year, but so many reports of various kinds are spread about that I never give credit to any of them. About three days ago it was known as a fact that we should remain here five years; today it is confidently asserted that we shall return to England without delay. They may send the weakest regiments home and compose new brigades; we are certainly not the weakest as we have the remnants of eight troops and the others only of six – our wounded men have likewise joined us from Brussels, amounting to about sixty. We have about a hundred and eighty men including these, out of which there are not more than a hundred and twenty effective, that is with horses and clothing, but there are a hundred horses at the depot, which if we remain here will of course be sent out. We have not had any remounts yet, nor shall for some time, I mean recruits, for these are scarce at present, and the two troops at the depot are but nominal ones, both together not exceeding twenty men; the hundred horses have all been recruited within the last month or two. About three troops of men out of the eight were totally destroyed, composed of fifty six each, and about five troops of horses; we had about an hundred men wounded, many of whom died, and many discharged unfit for service, and some sent home as being fit only for depot duty, so that if the regiment were now to go to England, I do not think we should muster more than two hundred effectives, and we disembarked at Ostend about four hundred and fifty men and horses, including officers. I believe this statement is pretty accurate. The Greys suffered more severely than we did, both in men and officers.'[2]

His hopes of returning home did not materialise. In December he wrote to his father: 'Nothing but bad news. Many dragoon regiments have received orders for marching homewards, among others the Life Guards and Blues, and where do you think they are going to send our miserable remains – to a village called Catoff [Le Cateau] on the frontier between Flanders and France, where it is likely we may remain some years. It is a most rascally hole; we bivouacked within a mile of it on our march, and we really could not then get water in it. There is no possible chance of general leave being granted this year. Tom will have nobody to shoot with him, neither will Broadheath resound with the reports of our guns after the Jacks [snipe] as I had once flattered myself. Lord Wellington has put a decided stop to all shooting; I should be risking my commission if I presumed to shoot a sparrow now to amuse myself. At Catoff, God knows, I have got a flute; paint brushes etc. I shall immediately provide myself with.'[2]

In early January 1816 Sergeant Major James Page wrote to his brother and sister in Bishop's Stortford: 'I have been long anxiously waiting to receive a letter from you; this is my second since I heard from you. I hope you will favour me with a few lines soon as convenient.

'It is finally settled for our Regiment to remain in France, the British Army (except that part which is now about returning to England) will remain on the frontiers of France three years, then, if nothing fresh happens, we shall return to England; our Regiment will be completed with horses from other Regiments which are returning to England; other things we shall have sent from England to us, such as arms, saddles etc. etc. to make us once more in fighting order. We have also many men and officers joined from England a few days ago, and about fifty men who are cured of wounds have joined us from Brussels.

'We shall march in a few days to a place called Baupaume, about sixty miles from Calais. The whole of the British Army will occupy the frontier towns.[13]

Whilst officers like John Hibbert were worrying about pay, leave and the ban on shooting, Sergeant Major Page was concerned with family worries. 'My wife has not joined me yet, nor cannot do till I can get her a passport. She came as far as Dover, but was obliged to return, no more soldiers wives being allowed to come over; the Duke of Wellington will allow only six to every hundred men. Our Colonel has promised to do what he can for me to procure a passport, and thinks he will succeed.

'I regret very much my wife did not join me immediately after our arriving at Rueil, it would have been many pounds in my pocket, but we expected above any Regiment to return to England, being so dreadfully pulled to pieces, but they are patching us up by degrees. I had a letter from Wm. Williams at Merton a few days ago; he says all the Collins are married, but Harry has no children. He is married himself, has one child, his sister and cousin are both married. Wm. and James Drinkwater are in the East Indies. My old master, Howard, I am sorry to hear, has failed. Little Dyer is dead – so you see there are some coming in the world and others going out, some rising and some falling.'

Page then goes on to express to his brother his feelings about army life. 'I often think how very fortunate you have been not to be so foolish as to come into the Army, although I have been in some respects very fortunate, yet I have had troubles that you are, and I hope ever will be, a stranger to.

'I am so fond of being in the Army in some respects that I should be sorry to leave it; my situation in it is a respectable one, but you see what troubles I am exposed to. No-one knows the soldier's troubles, fatigues and dangers but themselves. In regard to my wife and family, I could support them in a very comfortable manner, but I cannot get them to me, but have had to support them to so much disadvantage where the necessaries of life are so very dear to what they are in France, indeed I am very unhappy, though I make the best of it and all other troubles, always cherishing a hope for a change for the better.

'I hope you both, with your small family, enjoy good health, as, thank God, I do myself. We are now begun a New Year, that it may be enjoyed throughout in happiness and prosperity by you both, is the fervent wish of your affectionate brother – James Page. Address to me – "British Army in France", as I expect we shall move before you write to me again.'13

The Life Guards and Blues having returned to England, the King's Dragoon Guards were the sole remaining regiment of what had been the Household Cavalry Brigade. They were now sent to help form a new brigade. John Hibbert wrote to his sister on 13 December: 'We are now brigaded with the King's Own or Third Dragoons, and the Second Dragoon Guards, both regiments that have come from England within the last three months.'2 A hundred and forty–three years later the 1st King's Dragoon Guards and the 2nd Dragoon Guards (Queen's Bays) were to be joined more formally in a regimental amalgamation to form the present Regiment, 1st The Queen's Dragoon Guards.

Hibbert went on: 'Last Sunday we received the route to march to Neuilly Bridge on the following Thursday, about two miles from Paris, and occupy the quarters of the Life Guards, who were to evacuate them on that day, but a countermand arrived and therefore we are to remain in our present quarters until further orders. The whole army received a countermand, that is those who were destined to go to England – for what purpose, I do not know; I rather imagine a disturbance was expected in Paris. A continued scene of executions are going on there; Marshal Ney suffered very quietly – there was not the least disturbance during his execution. Many others whose names I do not know are daily executed.

'I am now in as good health as ever I was in my life and have no more occasion for my native air than I had this time last year. I am sorry to say that I have no more chance of going to England this year. The army is all very well as long as one is at home, but abroad it's no lounge, being no better than a school – If you please, Sir, will you permit me to sleep out of quarters tonight? – By no means, Sir – This is very pleasant. If I had one shilling for every time I have disobeyed this, I should be rich indeed, and every time I subject myself to be broke by a court-martial, but as to stopping in this infernal hole, Ruelle, it is not to be done; therefore when well, I spend half my time elsewhere. It is a hard case when a man cannot get one month's leave out of a year; notwithstanding all this I would not leave the service on any account whatever. There are few that are not attached to it, although you may hear them inveighing against it bitterly.'[2]

Officers and men were as ready to grumble as British soldiers ever have been, and often with good cause, but all their trials and difficulties could not extinguish their loyalty and obvious affection for their regiment.

. With peacetime soldiering, there also came changes of uniform. 'We are again changing our dress in every respect,' writes John Hibbert, 'except the jacket, and that is to be covered with a cuirass. The Life Guards are to be made cuirassiers, and those at home have already got them – a great pity! I think – for it gives a man no superiority as was evinced at the Battle of Waterloo where double the number of cuirassiers were killed when compared with our men. This will all be very expensive and will come hard upon those who have nothing but their pay to subsist on.

'I have no room for more, so Adieu.'[2]

So end John Hibbert's letters home. He was wrong insofar as

James Leatham, 1st King's Dragoon Guards.
Promoted Captain 19 July 1815.
Dressed in the new uniform and wearing his Waterloo Medal.

the King's Dragoon Guards and other regiments of Dragoon Guards were not burdened with cuirasses, but the Life Guards and Blues have worn them in full dress ever since.

On the 13 January 1816 the King's Dragoon Guards received their marching orders from Lieutenant Colonel Sir Charles Broke, the Deputy Quarter Master General. A copy of one such order survives – for a detachment of one officer, and three rank and file and three horses, commanded by Lieutenant John Hibbert. On 14 January they were to ride from Rouelle to Moiselles; on the 15th to Puiseux; on the 16th they were to reach Beauvais and the following day Marseille. The fifth day's march would take them to Poix, the sixth to Airaines, and finally on the seventh day, 20 January 1816, they were to arrive at Abbeville.[2] The regiment as a whole marched from Rouelle to the Department of the Pas de Calais where they went into extensive cantonments.[1]

In March 1816, thirty-seven King's Dragoon Guards were transferred from the regiment to the Mounted Staff Corps, and that month another troop was reduced at the depot in England. Also in March, there was a change of quarters and preparations began for the return to England of the eight KDG troops in France; 137 KDG horses were transferred to regiments that were to remain in France, and the depot in England received at the same time 118 from the 3rd Dragoons at Coventry. Before the regiment embarked, it was reviewed by Lieutenant General Lord Combermere, who praised both its gallantry in the field and its good conduct in quarters.[1]

Because of the distinguished services of the 1st King's Dragoon Guards during the campaign and especially its conduct at the Battle of Waterloo the regiment was allowed to commemorate its service by bearing the word 'Waterloo' on its standards and accoutrements. Every officer and man present at the battle received the Waterloo Medal, with the privilege of counting two years' service towards increments of pay and pension.[1]

The 1st King's Dragoon Guards disembarked at Dover on 7 May 1816 and marched to quarters around Hounslow. On 18 May they were reviewed on Hounslow Heath by the Duke of York, as a fitting end to an eventful year.[1]

Nothing symbolises that fierce regimental loyalty and comradeship more than the answer given to Captain Clark-Kennedy of the Royal Dragoons on 18th June 1815, when he called on those few horsemen returning from the first charge at Waterloo to form on him. 'We are King's Dragoon Guards – not Royals'; and they rode on.

Captain William Sterling,
1st King's Dragoon Guards

Sources

1 Cannon, R., *Historical Record of the First, or King's, Regiment of Dragoon Guards*, 1837.

2 Hibbert, Lieutenant John, 1st KDG, manuscript letters in possession of Lieutenant Colonel John Hibbert, The Light Infantry.

3 Naylor, Captain James, 1st KDG, manuscript diary in possession of 1st The Queen's Dragoon Guards' Museum.

4 *Cavalry Journal*, vol. 3, 1908. p. 154 (unattributed).

5 Mercer, General Cavalié, *Journal of the Waterloo Campaign*, 1927.

6 Crofton, Captain Sir Morgan, 'Household Cavalry and the Waterloo Campaign', *Household Brigade Magazine*, 1911.

7 Robson, Brian, *Swords of the British Army*, 1975.

8 Stanley, Private Charles, 1st KDG, manuscript letter in possession of the National Army Museum.

9 Siborne, Major General S. T., *Waterloo Letters*, 1891.

10 Page, Troop Sergeant Major James, 1st KDG. Letter published in *The KDG* (magazine), vol. 2, no. 5, June 1936.

11 *Cavalry Journal*, vol. 3, 1908. p. 156 (unattributed).

12 Kincaid, Captain Sir John, *Adventures in the Rifle Brigade*, 1830.

13 Page, Troop Sergeant Major James, 1st KDG. Letter published in *The KDG*, vol. 1, no. 5, May 1932.

14 Wheeler, Trumpeter Samuel, 1st KDG, 'The Battle of Waterloo', manuscript poem in the possession of Lieutenant Colonel John Hibbert, The Light Infantry.

15 Cotton, Sergeant Major Edward, 7th Hussars, *A Voice from Waterloo*, 1849.

16 Pericole, Ugo, *1815: The Armies at Waterloo*, 1973.

17 Cooper, Leonard, *British Regular Cavalry 1644–1914*, 1965.

18 Stubbings, Sergeant John, 1st KDG, manuscript letters in possession of Ernest Shead.

19 Cooke, J. T. C. and Shead, E., article in the *Journal of 1st The Queen's Dragoon Guards*, vol. 3, no. 7, 1979.

20 Manuscript documents in possession of relatives of Corporal John Dickson, Royal Scots Greys.

21 Houssaye, Henri, *1815: La Première Restauration, Le Retour de l'Ile d'Elbe et Les Cent Jours*, 1893.

22 Müffling, Baron C., *History of the Campaign in the Year 1815*, 1816.

23 Wallace, Captain Robert, 1st KDG, letter quoted by Siborne (see 9 above).

24 Chalfont, Lord, *Waterloo*, 1979.

25 *Journal of 1st The Queen's Dragoon Guards*, vol. 2, no. 5, 1977.

26 Howarth, David, *A Near Run Thing*, 1968.

27 Sutherland, John, *Men of Waterloo*, 1967.

28 Anglesey, Marquess of, *One-Leg*, 1961.

29 Alphabetical List of Killed and Wounded from the Official Returns, 1815.

30 Belfield, Eversley, *The Queen's Dragoon Guards*, 1978.

31 Fortescue, Sir John, *History of the British Army*, vol. 10, 1920.

32 Dalton's Waterloo Roll Call (*The Waterloo Call*), 1890.

33 Dwelley's Master Roll of Warrant Officers and Men. Public Record Office, WO 12/96.

34 Mint Medal Roll of Waterloo. Public Record Office. Mint 16/12.

35 Jones, George, *Battle of Waterloo*, 1817.

36 *Official Returns of the Strength and Loss of the British Army, 1815*.

37 *London Gazette Extraordinary*, 22 June 1815.

1st King's Dragoon Guards: Muster Roll, 1815

[for abbreviations, see end – p. 119]

OFFICERS

Lieutenant Colonel William Fuller k
Major Henry Graham k
Major John Bringhurst k
Captain Michael Turner w
Captain Battersby k
Captain James Naylor w
Captain John Sweeney w
Captain William Elton
Captain Robert Wallace w
Captain Thomas Quicke
Captain James Leatham
Captain William Stirling
Lieutenant Ralph Babbington
Lieutenant Robert Hawley
Lieutenant Thomas Brander

Lieutenant Edward Hamill
Lieutenant William Irvine w
Lieutenant Brooke k
Lieutenant J E Greaves
Lieutenant John Hibbert
Lieutenant George Quicke
Lieutenant Thomas Middleton
Adjutant Lieutenant Thomas
 Shelver k
Cornet The Hon H B Bernard k
Cornet William Huntley
Quarter Master John Brown
Surgeon J Goring
Asst Surgeon William Macauley
Asst Surgeon R A Pearson

NON-COMMISSIONED OFFICERS AND MEN

Abbotts, Jas.
Adams, Sgt John, cordwainer,
 Northampton
Adams, Corp John, labourer,
 Ipswich, sgt 25 Jy
Allen, Sgt John, k.
Andrews, John, w. dis. 27 Ja '17
Appleton, Wm., e. 22 De '05 a.17
Archbold, John, w. dis. 27 Ja '17
Arlett, John, k.
Arlingstall, Wm.

Armstrong, Wm.
Ashley, Robert
Ashton, John, e. 3 Oc '08
Ashton, John, e. 18 Jy '08. Flax-
 dresser Labenham
Ashworth, Sgt Tho., m.
Aspinal, Corp Geo. m.
Aston, Wm. w.
Atha, Benj., w. dis. 14 My

Babb, Henry

Bagley, Charles
Ball, Benj., dis. 4 No
Ball, Tho., e. 7 Mr '08, a. 17
Banks, Sgt John
Baptie, Alex.
Barber, John, c. 10 Au '05 a. 17; dis.
   12 Se '16
Barlow, Reg-Sgt-Maj Tho.
Barnett, Chas.
Barnett, Josh.
Barns, John, w.
Barrack, Wm., d. of w.
Barrell, Richard
Barrett, Tho., k.
Barron, John
Bartlemore, Tho., e. 16 Mr '13, a.
   17, w.
Bateman, Chas., k.
Bateman, Wm.
Battie, John
Battie, Tho., e. 25 Mr '00, a. 18. 28
   Lt. D., w.
Bearder, Jas., e. 31 Jy '05 a. 17
Beardsley, James
Beerson, Tho.
Bell, John
Bellinger, Benj., e. 25 Mr '00, a. 17,
   w. Hants F.C.
Benton, Wm., k.
Benwell, Trp-Sgt-Maj David, k.
Berkshire, Francis
Beeston, Samuel, w. dis. 31 Jy
Bewley, Hunter
Binder, Robert, w.
Birch, John
Birchell, Samuel, k.
Bird, Tho., k.
Blackburn, Henry
Blackhurst, Ralph
Blake, Tho.
Blanch, Corp Stephen, sgt 11 Fe; to
   staff c. of c.
Bodill, Edward
Bond, Edward

Bonser, Richard, k.
Booth, John, labourer, Seathorpe
Booth, John, labourer of Bolton, w.
Bossen, John, k.
Boswell, Tho.
Bottoms, Tho.
Bourne, Jas.
Bowen, Stephen, k.
Bower, Samuel, w. dis. 9 Fe '17
Bradbury, Sgt Emanuel
Bradbury, Geo.
Bradbury, John, k.
Bradshaw, Stamford
Bray, Tho.
Brew, Sgt Tho.
Bridge, Bury, w. dis. 31 Jy 1816
Bridge, James, e. 19 Ju '12, a. 16
Bridgeman, Wm., k.
Briggs, Abraham
Bright, Chas., e. 15 Mr '07, a.16
Briscoe, Corp Joseph, e. 15 Fe '12, a.
   17
Britney, John, d. of w. 7 Jy
Brockett, Wm., s. dis. 5 Fe 1817
Brooks, Benj., w. d.15 Ap
Brotherton, Tho., k.
Brown, Francis
Brown, James, labourer, Kitchens-
   well, k.
Brown, James, cottonspinner,
   Stockport, w.
Brown, John, labourer, Kitchens-
   well, e. 18 Oc 1794
Brown, John, taylor, St Peters, e. 18
   My '06, a. 16
Brown, John, e. 23 De '12, labourer,
   Basingstoke, k.
Brown, Richard
Brown, Sgt Wm., sawyer, Winches-
   ter
Bull, John, k.
Bull, Samuel
Bullman, Corp Geo., k.
Bunny, Wm., staff c. of c.

Butcher, John
Butterworth, Edmund, Norforlk
F.C., e. 1 Jy '03, k.
Buxton, James, k.

Caplin, Wm., k.
Capon, Henry, e. 8 Ju '99, a. 17,
  staff c. of c.
Carr, Patrick, k.
Carter, Isaac, staff c. of c.
Carter, John, k.
Carter, Josh.
Castle, Sgt Josh.
Chantry, Geo., w.
Chaplin (Chapman), Wm., e. 8 May
  '12, a. 16
Chapple, Henry
Chelton, John
Chiney, John, dis. 2 De '16
Chivers, Sgt Wm.
Chorley, Samuel, k.
Clapp, Jos.
Clark, John, blacksmith, Thetford
Clark, Corp John, w. e. 11 De '09, a.
  17, cabinet maker, Liberton
Clark, Corp Wm., w.
Clegg, Jas., k.
Clements, Tho., Somerset F.C., e. 13
  Au '00
Cockburn, Tho. 29 L.D., k.
Collingham, Jas.
Cook, John, k.
Cook, Josh,
Cook, Samuel
Cooper, Jeremiah
Cooper, Sgt James
Copley, Geo., k.
Coult, Tho., w.
Cousens, Wm.
Cracknell, Robert, w. sent to Eng.
  6 Jy, re-joined 17 De '15, dis.
  De '16
Craig, Robert, k.
Crane, John, k.

Crosby, Wm., e. 30 Au '13, a. 16yrs
  73 dys.
Crosswell, John
Cullam, Geo., w.
Culley, Wm., w. dis. 21 Ju 1816
Cumner, Charles
Curtice, Jas., k.
Custobody, James

Dakin, Tho., e. 16 Ju '10, a. 17
Dale, Tho.
Dalrymple, Robert, Lanark F.C.
Davenport, Adam, e. 11 My '12, a.
  16
Davenport, Tho., dis. 21 Ju
Davis, Geo., e. 6 Mr '13, a. 17yrs
  311 dys
Davis, James, w.
Davis, Richard, k.
Deacon, Robert, staff c. of c.
Deakin, Tho., w. dis 27 Ja 1817
Death, Jas., e. 4 Fe '07, a. 15
Death, Trump Wm.
Denner, David
Derry, John, e. 18 Au '10, a. 17
Dixon, Geo., k.
Dixon, Trump-Maj Wm.
Docker, John, w.
Dolton, Wm.
Dowanham, John, e. 28 Jy '12, a. 16
Downing, F.D. m. dis. 6 Mr
Drake, Sgt Josh,
Dry, John, w.
Dudgeon, Corp Tho., k.
Dymes, John, k.
Dyson, Ely

Eekley, Tho., w.
Elliott, W., e. 12 Oc '06, a. 17
Ellis, Esau
Elson, Tho.
Emerson, John, e. 21 Jy '10, a. 17
Englefield, Josh,
Evans, James 4th Ft.

Evans, Luke, k.
Evett, Wm. k.

Fairbrother, Wm.
Fairclough, Trp-Sgt-Maj James
Fairfax, Josh, e. 24 Fe '11, a. 16
Falconbridge, John, w.
Fieldhouse, Samuel, e. 21 Jy '01, a. 17
Fitch, Wm., w.
Fletcher, James, Rutland F.C. staff c. of c. 25 Mr
Folkes, Wm.
Frankum, John
Fray, Wm. w. York hospital, Chelsea
Freeman, Joshua
Fulbrook, John, k.
Fuller, John, e. 13 My '12, a. 17

Gadsby, Wm., e 30 Ju '12, a. 16
Gardiner, Timothy
Garratt, Sgt Tho., k.
Gaskill, Tho., e. 17 Oc '12, a. 16
Gee, Peter
Gibbons, Samuel, dis. 27 Ja '17
Gieves, Henry
Gillon, Chas., d. of w. 29 Ju '15
Glover, John, k.
Godber, Henry, k.
Goodacre, Corp Wm., sgt 11 Fe '16
Gordon, Chas., k.
Green, Jeremiah
Green, Corp Richard
Greenhalgh, James, crofter, of Bolton
Greenhalgh, Jas., bleacher of Bolton, w.
Greenhalgh, Richard, w.
Gregory, Joseph, e. 13 Oc '05, a. 16
Greyshon, John, staff c. of cav. 25 Mr
Grimshaw, Tho.,
Gripton, Corp Robert

Groves, Edward, k.
Groves, Wm., e. 23 Au '10 a. 17
Guilford, Tho.

Haiste, Geo.
Hale, Richard, k.
Hall, Francis, d. of w. 19 No '15
Hall, Richard
Hall Richard
Hall, Robert, w.
Halson, Armr.-Sgt Edmund
Hancock, John, k.
Hansler, Chas.
Hardsman, Richard, e. 7 Ja '12, a. 15
Harfield, Joseph, k.
Harriman, Benj., w.
Harris, Lewis, d. of w. 14 Au '15
Harris, Richard, w.
Harrison, Samuel
Harrison, Wm., k.
Hasker, Tho., w.
Haslam, Wm.
Hawkins, Josh.
Hawkyard, Tho.
Haynes, Chas.
Haynes, Matthew, k.
Haywood, Corp Chas.
Headings, John, k.
Headley, Robert, dis. 21 Ja '17
Heap, Wm., w.
Helps, Leonard, dis. 26 Ap 1816
Hemming, Edward, dis. 27 Fe '17
Hemming, Corp Wm.
Herbert (Herbett), Tho., e. 6 No '00, a. 16
Hewett, Matthew
Hewkin, Tho., k.
Hickman, Wm.
Hill, Geo., k.
Hill, James, w. 5 R. Vet. B. 8 No
Hill, Ramage, w. to do. 4 De
Hill, Robert, Norfolk F.C.
Hillier, Trump Wm.

Holdknow, Samuel, e. 26 Jy '12, a. 17

Hollis, Sgt Richard, adj. 8 Jy '36, lieut. 12 Ja '38, lt. R. Can R. 24 Oc '45, d. Canada ret. capt. '56

Holloway, Moses

Holmes, Sgt Jas., m.

Holmes, John, e. 23 My '09, a. 15

Houghton, Josh., w. dis. 27 Ja '17

Houghton, Payr-Sgt Rich.

Howarth, Chas.

Horobin, Samuel, e. 15 De '11, a. 17

Howett, Wm.

Hurford, Corp Robert

Hurford, Wm., w.

Hutchins, Robert, k.

Hutchinson, Jas., e. 5 Jy '12, a 17

Jacques, Francis, e. 8 Fe '18, a. 16 yrs. 254 dys.

James, John, labourer of Selstone, e. 5 Mr '08

James, John, e. 25 Mr '11, w. dis. 21 Ju '16, nailer, Roscommon

James, Geo.

James, Wm., staff c. of c., 25 Mr

Jennings, Corp John

Jepson, Josh.

Johnson, Eml., e. 29 Jy '05, a. 17

Johnson, Moses, k.

Johnson, Wm., blacksmith of Kirby-under-dale, e. 1 Au '09

Johnson, Wm., blacksmith of Bils-don, e. 12 My '07, k.

Jones, John, k.

Jones, Richard, w.

Jones, Tho.

Jones, Wm.

Kay, John, weaver, Manchester, w.

Kay, John, weaver, Bury, e. 1 Oc '12, a. 17½

Kennett, Sgt Richard

Kibble, Samuel, k.

Kibble, Corp Tho., e. 9 Se '07, a. 16, sgt 11 Fe '16, w.

Kilband, Wm.

King, Josh., d. of w. in Eliz. Hosp. 22 Ju

Kisbie, Tho., w.

Kitchen, Robert, k.

Knight, Geo.

Ladd, Geo., w.

Lamport, John, dis. 6 Mr

Lancely, Wm., e. 22 Fe '09 a. 17, w.

Lawdemore, Henry, k.

Lawson, Jonathan, to staff c. of c. 25 Mr

Lawson, Wm., dis. 16 Ja '17

Leadley, Jas., k.

Lee, John, k.

Lee, Thos.

Lee, Wm.

Leek, John

Lenton, Wm., e. 30 Mr '06, a. 15

Levers, Timothy

Levitt, Isaac

Levitt, Trp-Sgt-Maj John

Lewis, John, k.

Lewis, Josh., e. 29 Ju '08, a. 16

Linton, Trp-Sgt-Maj, Tho.

Lloyde, Tho., w.

Lock, Jas., dis. 9 Ja '17

Lockey, Henry

Lomax, Josh., e. 12 Ap '11, a. 15

Lomax, Wm.

Long, Josh., k.

Longfield, Wm.

Lord, Chas.

Lord, Jas., k.

Loughton, John, k.

Lynn, Thompson, k.

Lywood, Joshua, w.

McKay, Alex.

McKenna, Jas., k.

Maiden, John
Makin, Josh.
Marnham, Michael, k.
Marsden, Geo.
Marshall, Geo., e. 28 No '08, a. 16
Martin, Jas.
Martin, Wm., e. 2 Ju '06, a. 16
Marvin, Wm., e. 2 Ju '06, a. 16
Mason, Tho., e. 22 Se '12, a. 17
Mason, Tho., e 24 Se '12, k.
Mather, Jas., e. 16 Se '12, a. 17
Mathews, Robert, e. 6 Ja '06, a. 17, s.
May, Richard, dis. 12 Ja '17
Meyrick, John, dis. 17 No 1816
Millett, John, w.
Missett, Saddr-Sgt Robert
Moass, Josh., e. 9 Mr '13, a. 17 yrs 92 dys
Monger, Josh., to staff c. of c. 18 Oc '16
Morley, Josh.
Morley, Wm., k.
Morton, Eml.
Moss, Benj., w., dis. 7 Ja '17
Musson, Jas., e. 24 Mr '07, a. 17
Mutton, Sgt Henry

Newbold, Wm., k.
Newell, Mark, k.
Newman, Edward, k.
Newton, Wm., e. 17 Ja '09, a. 17
Nicholson, Henry
Nicholson, Tho., w.
Nickson, James
Norman, Sgt Nathl., m.
Nosely, John
Novis, Tho., w.
Noyes, Septimus
Nuttall, Sgt James
Nuttall, John, spinner, Bury, e. 14 Mr '13, k.
Nuttall, John, e. 25 Ap '09, w.,

cotton spinner, Prestwick, to staff c. of c.
Nuttall, Sgt, Robert, w.

Oliver, Trump Wm., hairdresser, Brighton
Oliver, Wm., labourer, Bps., Waltham
Orme, Jas., e 31 Jy '13, a. 16
Osborne, Trump Wm., w.
Ovendale, Corp Geo.
Owen, Josh, w.
Ozwin, Corp John, sgt. 25 De

Page, Trp-Sgt-Maj James
Page, Corp James, labourer, Redman, sgt 25 Se
Parker, John, k.
Parr, Corp John
Partridge, Tho.
Pattinson, Wm.
Pearson, John, k.
Peat, John
Peat, Wm.
Pegg, Josh.
Pemberton, Tho.
Perkins, Nathl., w. dis. 30 De '16
Perkins, Corp Tho., sgt 25 Mr to staff c. of c.
Perry, John, to staff c. of c. 19 Oc '16
Pilgrim, James
Picton, John, w. dis. 17 Ja '27
Pigg, Wm., w. dis. 4 De '16
Pinder, John, k.
Pink, Chas.
Pink, Wm, e. 4 De '12, a. 17yrs 274 dys
Piper, Isaac, k.
Piper, Wm.
Pizzey, Richard,
Platt, Josh.
Pointon, Sgt Tho.
Pointon, Wm.
Pomfrey, Chas., Rutl'd F.C.

Poole, John, dis. 5 De '16
Pope, James
Porter, Richard, e. 13 Jy '11, a. 16
Porter, Wm.
Postell, John
Poultney, Josh., staff c. of c.
Powell, Jas., dis. 31 Jy '16 3rd Dns.
Preece, Benj.
Preece, Philip
Preece, Tho., w.
Price, Edward, w.
Priece, Tho.
Purham, Giles, staff c. of c. 19 Oc '16

Ramsden, Jas., k.
Ramsden, Tho., k.
Raynor, Geo.
Reed, Jas.
Reeves, John
Reeves, Tho.
Rhodes, Edmund, e. 11 My '12, a. 15
Richards, Abm.
Richardson, John, labourer, Colledge, k.
Richardson, Sgt John, carpenter, Throsenby
Richardson, Wm., w., dis. 27 Au '17
Rider, John, F.W.K. of Loughborough, e. 29 No '06, a. 17
Rider, John, labourer of Barrow-on-Soar, w. dis. 19 Ja '17, e. 20 Ja '07
Rider, Tho., e. 10 Ju '10, a. 17, w.
Ridge, Jas.
Ringland, Sgt Robert
Robinson, John
Robinson, Tho., weaver, Manchester
Robinson, Tho., F.W.K. of Desboro
Robinson, Wm., e. 22 Jy '13, a. 17
Roe, Samuel
Rollinson, Corp Jas., w. sgt. 10 Fe, staff c. of c. 25 Mr

Roper, Corp Ralph
Ross, Elias, k.
Rosthorn, Edward, w.
Rosthorn, Henry, k.

Sacker, Chas., e. 17 De '00, a. 17
Sanderson, Wm., k.
Sands, Sgt Tho.
Sarson, Wm., w. dis. 13 Oc '16
Saunt, James, k.
Schofield, John, w.
Schofield, Wm., to staff c. of cav.
Scott, James, e. 26 Jy '11 a. 17
Seagrave, Wm. dis. 6 Mr '17
Seaman, Stephen
Serjeant, John, d. of w. 6 Se
Settle, Wm.
Sharp, James, k.
Sharpless, John
Sharpley, James, w.
Shaw, John, w.
Sheffield, John, e. 19 No '09, a. 16
Sheward, Sgt, Wm.
Shipman, John
Shirley, Wm., w.
Sikes, Josh.
Simpson, Corp James, w. to staff c. of cav. 25 Ap
Simpson, John, w.
Simpson, Henry
Simpson, Tho., k.
Sims, John, k.
Sims, Silas, w.
Sisson, Samuel, w.
Sisson, Corp John, e. 29 Ju '05, a. 17
Slater, Geo.
Smallwood, Sgt Nathl., m. rejoined later
Smith, John
Smith, Josh., dis. 5 De '16
Smith, Sgt Samuel, labourer, Romford,
Smith, Samuel, cordwainer, Woodford, dis. 4 Ja '17

Smith, Tho.
Smith, Sgt Wm.
Snutch, John, e. 15 Fe '09, a. 17
Soper, Robert
Speller, Corp James
Stacey, James, k.
Staniland, Reuben, e. 5 Mr '08, a. 17
Stanley, Chas., k.
Starkey, Richard
Starbrook, Josh.
Starkey, Sgt Chas., m.
Steel, James, Lanark F.C.
Stevens, Geo., corp 18 Ju
Stevenson, Leonard
Stokes, John, w. dis. 5 De '16
Stoneystreet, John, w. dis. 31 Jy '16, e. 25 Ja '06, a. 17
Storey, James
Street, John
Stringer, Corp Tho., w., sgt 19 Ju
Stubbings, Sgt John
Suttcliff, Josh., w., e. 29 Ap '01, a. 16
Sutton, John
Sutton, Wm., e. 30 Ju '07, a. 16
Syer, Stephen, k.

Tanner, Francis
Tasker, John
Taylor, Geo.
Taylor, Corp Tho., a. 17 on 12 Ja '00
Taylor, Wm., e. 15 Ja '12, a. 17
Tebbs, Sgt John, m.
Temple, John, 1st L. Gds, e. 12 Mr '08, k.
Thomas, Schoolmr-Sgt John
Thompson, Corp Geo.
Thompson, Jas.
Thornton, Jas.
Thwaites, John
Tilley, Samuel
Timpson, Tho., k.

Towers, Jas.
Tracey, Trp-Sgt-Maj John, w.
Tressler, Corp Wm., e. 14 Ju '06, a. 15, dis. 27 Ja '17
Trilloe, Geo., k.
Tucker, Sgt John Lewis
Tucker, Samuel, w. dis. 21 Ju '16
Tudman, Jas., w. dis. 2 No on account of wounds
Tune, John, w.
Turner, Sgt Wm.
Tyers, Tho.

Valance, Wm. w.
Varley, Wm.
Vent, Sgt Tho., m.
Vickers, Jas.
Vickers, Wm., to staff c. of c. 25 Mr
Vincent, John, e 22 Jy '08, a. 17

Wainford, Henry
Wakefield, Tho., d. of w. 25 Ju
Walkden, Adam, d. 8 Jy '16
Walker, Chas., labourer, Farley Hill
Walker, Edward, k.
Walker, Geo., e. 2 Jy '12, a. 17
Walker, John, labourer, Farley Hill, w. dis. 27 Ja '17
Waldron, John
Wale, John
Wale, Wm., w.
Warbutton, Tho., k.
Warcop, Jas.
Ward, Sgt John
Ward, Mathew
Ward, Nathl., w., e. 2 De '11, a. 17
Ward, Sam., e. 25 Fe '06, a. 16
Ward, Wm. w.
Warren, Edward, k.
Warren, John
Warren, Richard, e. 25 Ju '08, a. 16
Watkins, Josh., k.
Watts, Corp Richard, sgt 30 Se
Watts, Corp Robt., sgt 19 Ju

Watts, Trump Wm.
Webster, Richard, k.
Webster, Sam., e. 23 Au '01, a. 17
West, Job, w.
West, John, e. 12 Au '06, a. 16, to staff c. of c. 25 Mr
Westroop, Josh.
Wheatcroft, John, dis. 20 Mr '17
Wheeler, Trump Saml.
White, Henry
White, John, w.
White, Josh.
White, Saml., w.
White, Corp Tho., w., dis. 3 De
White, Wm., w.
Whitehead, Richard, to staff c. of c. 25 Mr
Whitehouse, Wm., dis. on account of wounds 6 Mr
Wild, Edward, w.
Wilkins, Trump Robert, w.
Wilkins, Tho., k.
Williamson, Richard, w., dis. 27 Ja '17

Williams, Wm., k., labourer, Guildford
Willshee, Wm., k.
Wilson, Sgt Jonathan, w.
Witton, John
Wood, Josh.
Wood, Richard, w.
Woodburn, Wm.
Woodman, Tho., k.
Woodward, Jas.
Woodward, Wm., w. to 5 R. Veteran Batt. 25 De '15
Woon, Tho.
Wright, Trp-Sgt-Maj Edward, m.
Wright, John, F.W.K. Birmingham, e. 15 Oc '04 k.
Wright, John, labourer, Upper Ottery, e. 8 Oc '03, a. 17, w.
Wright, Jonathan
Wyatt, Ath., w., dis. 27 Ja 1817

Young, John to staff c. of cav. 25 Mr
Young, Wm.

The following men, whose trades and birth-places are given in pay-list W. O. 12/96 were *not* at Waterloo.

> Richardson, Sgt John, carpenter, Troxenby
> Simpson, Thomas, labourer, Churchgarforth
> Simpson, Thomas, labourer, Wooton
> Turner, Robert, F.W.K. Skegby
> Turner, Robert, weaver, Rochdale
> Walker, John, labourer, Dumfries
> Williams, William, F.W.K. Littlethorp
> Williams, William, labourer, Longthorpe

ABBREVIATIONS: a. age on enlistment; b. born; c. of f. commander of the forces; d. died; d. of w. died of Waterloo wounds; dis. discharged; d. & r. discharged & recommended; e. enlisted in this corps; F.C. Fencible Cavalry; F.I. Fencible Infantry; FWK Framework Knitter; i. inv. invalided to England; k. killed at Waterloo; m. missing; s. sick; t. number of troop; w. wounded at Waterloo.

Index

121